The practice of entrepreneurship

The practice of entrepreneurship

Geoffrey G. Meredith
Robert E. Nelson
Philip A. Neck

INTERNATIONAL LABOUR OFFICE
GENEVA

ISBN 92-2-102846-1 (limp cover)
ISBN 92-2-102839-9 (hard cover)

First published 1982

Photocomposed in India
Printed in Switzerland

This book is intended mainly for practising managers, would-be entrepreneurs and management advisers who are interested in developing entrepreneurial skills.

Although the International Labour Office has been promoting entrepreneurship development for some time, *The practice of entrepreneurship* is its first publication on the subject. It has been written by three authors who feel that it fills a gap in management development literature. What is contained in the book can be demonstrated practically and is supported by relevant research.

The work is in three parts. Part I deals with the internal or personal characteristics and behavioural traits of entrepreneurs. Part II refers specifically to financial aspects of entrepreneurship in which business success is most commonly reflected. Part III is about the external aspects of entrepreneurship, such as dealing with people able to help entrepreneurs.

Geoffrey G. Meredith is Director of the Financial Management Research Centre, University of New England, Armidale, New South Wales (Australia); Philip A. Neck, formerly Chief of the Small Enterprise Development Section, Management Development Branch, International Labour Office, Geneva (Switzerland), is Director of the ILO Office in New Delhi (India); and Robert E. Nelson is Chairman of the Division of Business Education, University of Illinois, Urbana, Ill. (United States). All three authors are professional management consultants and trainers who have worked with entrepreneurs in a wide range of occupations, covering services, trade and industry in rural and urban settings. They also consider themselves to be relatively entrepreneurial. Their work with the International Labour Office and other agencies has allowed them to work in industrialised and developing countries throughout Africa, the Americas, Asia, Europe, the Middle East and Oceania. What is discussed in this book is a distillation of their research and readings, as well as their personal experiences and involvement with entrepreneurs and those who deal with entrepreneurs.

The authors acknowledge their indebtedness and express their thanks to those colleagues, entrepreneurs, researchers and others who have helped to make this publication possible.

CONTENTS

PERSONAL CHARACTERISTICS OF ENTREPRENEURS

Being entrepreneurial means combining personal characteristics, financial means and resources within your environment. Each entrepreneur has unique characteristics, and it is the purpose of Part I to identify some of these characteristics. All entrepreneurs have their own individual styles of owning and managing their businesses. However, there are many personal characteristics you may want to develop which can help your business to become successful.

Part I includes:
1. Being entrepreneurial
2. Leadership
3. Risk-taking
4. Decision-making
5. Business planning
6. Using time effectively

Part I deals with those personal characteristics which help entrepreneurs to be successful. Most people have the capacity to exhibit these personal entrepreneurial characteristics; however, it is the entrepreneurial type of person who is able to take action to use these characteristics at work to achieve business success.

Being entrepreneurial is having the ability to find and evaluate opportunities, gather the necessary resources and implement action to take advantage of these opportunities. Entrepreneurs are leaders and they must exhibit leadership qualities in conducting most of their activities. They take calculated risks and enjoy challenges that involve moderate risks.

Entrepreneurs strongly believe in themselves and in their ability to make good decisions. It is this decision-making ability that is a distinguishing mark of entrepreneurs.

Entrepreneurs must spend a great deal of time in planning business activities. As their business grows, the greater is the need for planning.

Time is something that cannot be saved, but time is something that must be used wisely. Entrepreneurs need to manage their time effectively, and the key to using time effectively is through better management.

The six chapters in Part I highlight many of the personal aspects of entrepreneurs with which most people can identify, and which can be developed over a period of time. Read these chapters with the understanding that you *can* take control of the personal aspects of your life to make your work more productive and more entrepreneurial. Understanding that the personal aspects of your life can have positive effects on your business activities should give you the incentive and motivation to develop your personal entrepreneurial characteristics to the fullest extent.

BEING ENTREPRENEURIAL

1

Entrepreneurs are people who have the ability to see and evaluate business opportunities; to gather the necessary resources to take advantage of them; and to initiate appropriate action to ensure success

Entrepreneurs are action-oriented, highly motivated individuals who take risks to achieve goals. The following list of characteristics and traits provides a working profile of entrepreneurs:[1]

Characteristic	Trait
Self-confidence	Confidence
	Independence, individuality
	Optimism
Task-result oriented	Need for achievement
	Profit-oriented
	Persistence, perseverence, determination
	Hard work, drive, energy
	Initiative
Risk-taker	Risk-taking ability
	Likes challenge
Leadership	Leadership behaviour
	Gets along well with others
	Responsive to suggestions, criticisms
Originality	Innovative, creative
	Flexible (openness of mind)
	Resourceful
	Versatile, knowledgeable
Future-oriented	Foresight
	Perceptive

[1] This list was prepared at a workshop on entrepreneurship conducted at the East-West Center, Honolulu, in 1977.

3

The list includes traits that you should possess, or have potential to develop, if you wish to be entrepreneurial. You may not need *all* these traits; but the more you have, the greater chance there is of your being an entrepreneur.

It should be stressed that many of these traits are highly inter-related: that is, people who are self-confident will probably accept responsibility for their own decisions, be willing to take risks, and become leaders.

Not all entrepreneurs are alike, either in these 19 traits or in their personal qualities. Often, they differ markedly from each other: some are aloof and arrogant; some are warm and friendly; some are withdrawn and shy. But when measured on various personal traits and skills it is clear that, *as a group*, entrepreneurs differ substantially from non-entrepreneurs.

> It is unlikely that you will ever meet an entrepreneur who rates high on all 19 traits; but it is very likely that the entrepreneurs you do meet will rate high on most of them, especially self-confidence, risk-taking ability, flexibility, a strong need to achieve, and a strong desire to be independent

ENTREPRENEURIAL PHILOSOPHY

To some extent, success as an entrepreneur depends on your willingness to accept responsibility for your own work. You must learn a great deal about yourself if you intend to pursue goals which are compatible with what you most want in life. Your power comes from your own actions rather than the actions of others. Even though the risk of failure is always present, entrepreneurs take risks by assuming responsibility for their actions. Failure must be accepted as a learning experience. Some entrepreneurs succeed only after experiencing many failures. Learning from past experiences will help to channel your actions to obtain more positive results, and success will result from persistent efforts.

Pursue goals related to your skills and abilities. Accept yourself as you are, and try to emphasise your strengths and play down your weaknesses. If you pursue these goals honestly and aggressively, you are likely to achieve positive results. Being goal-oriented will bring out your best qualities. Engage in activities which are important to you and which you do best.

Most people do not recognise the broad scope they have for determining their actions. Achieving perfection is an ideal in attaining a goal but it is not a realistic objective for most entrepreneurs. Acceptable results are more important than perfect results. Trying to achieve perfect results for one goal over too long a time will only prevent your personal growth and development.

THE ENTREPRENEUR AS A PERSON

Every person is a unique individual, and no two persons are alike. All people have had different past experiences, are living in different life situations, have different commitments and responsibilities, and have different life goals.

The previous experiences of an entrepreneur are usually broad and varied and determine his present life situation. Most entrepreneurs have modelled themselves on another, probably older, entrepreneur; and close identification with such a "role model" will lead to the acquisition of entrepreneurial behaviour and skills.

Your current job and your financial and family circumstances, as well as other factors, help to determine your attitudes towards being entrepreneurial. You have various obligations and commitments to yourself and to others, including your spouse, family, employer or employees, friends, and other community members. If you have too many commitments and responsibilities outside your work, you will find it difficult to be entrepreneurial. In planning for the future, be realistic in determining those things about yourself that can be changed and those that cannot. Your past experiences should help you to understand better your present situation.

Most entrepreneurs have definite goals and expectations. The clearer your goals are, the more likely you are to achieve them. The first column in the chart in figure 1 lists some life factors, a consideration of which will enable you to gain a better understanding of who you are and where you are going. The next three columns will help to determine your desired goals for each factor; your current situation regarding each goal; and your plans for achieving each goal.

The list of entrepreneurial life factors on the chart is not complete, and you should add other items. By completing the chart, you will be better able to view yourself as an integrated person. The more you can integrate your various life goals, the better entrepreneur you will be.

You must be willing to learn from experience and change with the times. You must constantly be aware of new ways to increase your own productivity. One of the main keys to your success is your involvement in continuous personal growth

Figure 1. Entrepreneurial Life Factors Chart

Factor	Desired goal	Current situation	Plans for achieving goal
Career advancements			
Business improvement			
Financial affairs			
Physical well-being			
Education			
Family			
Recreation			
Business associates			
Friendships			
Community service			
Self-improvement			
Business opportunities			
Security			
Other:			

BEING ENTREPRENEURIAL IN YOUR CAREER

Being an entrepreneur is more than a job or a career: it is a life-style, and certain principles may influence your career strategy for being an entrepreneur. You must be flexible and imaginative, be able to plan, take risks, make decisions and implement action to achieve your goals. You should be realistic as well as future-oriented. You should be willing to work under conditions of conflict, change and ambiguity. This will require that you analyse yourself in relation to the environment in which you will have to work.

Your career objectives should be stated in terms of priorities, and the intended outcomes should be related to measurable and meaningful goals. These objectives should be challenging, and should motivate you to learn and grow in your career. You learn best when doing things which interest you, and when you are committed to specific goals.

You should look at your personal qualities in a realistic manner. Your responses to the following questions will give some indication of your entrepreneurial abilities and of the type of person you are:

☐ Does your work require you to be self-reliant?

☐ Are you usually self-motivated to achieve goals?

☐ Do you work well with other people?

☐ Within a group of people, do you usually assume a leadership role?

☐ Do you take advantage of opportunities to expand your own knowledge through reading and through attending educational courses?

☐ Are you able to communicate well with others?

☐ Are you a good listener?

☐ Do your accomplishments indicate that you are growing personally and professionally?

☐ Do you have a positive self-image?

☐ What goals do you want to achieve and are these goals challenging?

☐ Do you make decisions easily and confidently?

An important feature of being entrepreneurial is that you provide something of value to others. The greater the need people have for your product or service, the greater your rewards will be. If you work to help other people, to raise their standards of living and to improve their lives, you will be serving the needs of society. This is the meaning of being an entrepreneur

---

CAREER ATTITUDES

Entrepreneurs have certain abilities which apply to a wide range of careers. Thinking about the following factors will help you to develop entrepreneurial attitudes toward your career:

☐ Select a career which will allow you freedom to express yourself creatively as well as permit personal and professional growth. Don't underestimate your own abilities and talents.

☐ When setting out on your career, pattern your actions after successful persons who are in the same kind of occupation. Once you understand their techniques for achieving success, use them to develop your own career in your own way—don't follow them slavishly. Concentrate on specific aspects of these successful people. Develop positive traits through practice on a day-to-day basis.

☐ Know as much about your chosen career as possible. This knowledge will help you to become an expert in that particular type of work.

☐ Always try to improve. Be satisfied with past accomplishments, but look to the future to create new goals as a source of self-improvement.

☐ Because everything is constantly changing, you must change also. Accept change and use it to motivate you to achieve higher-level goals.

☐ Be action-oriented. It is through action that you are able to take advantage of new career opportunities which will lead to future success.

☐ Have a good understanding of your personal strengths and weaknesses. Rather than spending time eliminating weaknesses, highlight and use your strengths. Recognise your weaknesses, and use other resources to compensate for these deficiencies.

☐ Follow a routine in your daily activities to allow yourself more time to be entrepreneurial. Less energy is used in routine activities, whereas non-routine activities require more time and energy. Introducing order and routine into your daily life will allow you more energy for creative, entrepreneurial activities.

☐ When personally involved, accept responsibility for seeing that the activity will be successful. Realistically accept the responsibilities as well as the restrictions of a situation.

☐ Be able to combine the unique qualities of individuals working for you to obtain maximum benefits. Your success is influenced by the performance of your employees.

☐ Exhibit confidence in yourself and your employees. You should be confident in the abilities of your staff and in the results they achieve.

☐ Your personal appearance will affect your self-image. If you look good, you will probably feel good. Depending upon your appearance, other people may react to you in a positive or negative manner. To improve both your self-concept and the impression other people have of you, make sure your appearance is appealing.

☐ Making decisions is an essential quality of successful entrepreneurs. In most cases, decisions have to be made with limited facts and information. When a situation requires a decision to be made, you must be ready: you must make the decision *and* see that it is acted upon.

☐ Live in the present and waste no time reliving past failures. Look to the future to provide rewarding and satisfying experiences.

> The biggest asset to sustaining entrepreneurial ability is a positive attitude. In addition, determination, experience, persistence and just plain hard work are essential to being a successful entrepreneur

MENTAL ATTITUDES

Entrepreneurs have a sound mental outlook on life. They are mature individuals who have developed a way of viewing all experiences in a healthy manner. The following suggestions will help you to develop good mental attitudes:

☐ Entrepreneurs are people who know how to find satisfaction in work and are proud of their accomplishments. Exhibit a positive mental attitude towards your work, because it is this attitude which will help to determine your success.

☐ Your mind is a powerful tool. Setting aside a certain time each day for reflective thinking will allow your mind to be engaged in thoughtful activities.

☐ Most people limit their thoughts to their day-to-day problems and activities. Use your imagination to expand your thoughts and think "big". Persons who see the "big picture" are the ones who are entrepreneurial and are potential business and community leaders.

☐ Having a sense of humour helps to maintain a healthy mental attitude. Being too serious can be unhealthy and detrimental to your work. Exhibiting a sense of humour affects others by spreading optimism and a relaxed atmosphere.

☐ Mentally, you must be highly organised, and be able to focus on a variety of problems. You should be able to move your attention from one problem area to another with a minimum of effort.

The right mental attitude towards work is extremely important. Successful entrepreneurs enjoy their work and are totally dedicated to what they are doing. Their positive mental attitudes turn their jobs into exciting, interesting and rewarding work

---

IMPORTANCE OF ATTITUDES

Most people let conditions control their attitudes, whereas entrepreneurs use their attitudes to control conditions. A positive mental attitude helps you to focus on desired activities and events and on the results you hope to achieve. Even negative experiences will contain something positive. You must have a positive mental attitude towards all events and look for benefits from every experience.

A positive mental attitude is developed over a long period of time. The following factors are useful to entrepreneurs in developing a positive mental attitude:

☐ Concentrate only on being involved in positive activities.

☐ Select positive objectives in your work.

☐ Associate with people who think and act in an entrepreneurial manner. It is probable that you will acquire some of the thinking, mannerisms and characteristics of the people around you.

☐ Avoid negative thoughts and ideas.

☐ Recognise that you control your mind and use it productively.

☐ Be constantly alert for opportunities to improve your situation, whether it be your personal life, work life, or life in the community.

☐ Don't be afraid to give up an idea if it is not producing the right results. It is better to change direction than to pursue an idea that is not working out satisfactorily.

☐ The environment in which you live will affect your performance. If your environment is not appropriate to your needs, change it; or move to another environment which is more positive and conducive to achieving desirable goals.

☐ Believe in yourself and your talents. Success comes to those who have faith in their own abilities and use their abilities to the fullest extent.

☐ Relieve mental stress by taking action. Focus your thoughts on a specific problem. Once you have reached a decision, take action to solve the problem. Try to resolve mental conflicts as quickly as possible.

With respect to this last point, recent research suggests that a key attribute of successful entrepreneurs is the ability to make good decisions while under stress. Managing during continuing stress situations calls for good mental and physical condition. Much has been written on this subject. The essentials for handling stress include: moderation in eating and drinking; sufficient rest and exercise; abstinence from smoking; separating the "important" from the "urgent" from the "other" things to do, then tackling the "important" issues first by committing yourself to *action* rather than worry; working out contingency plans to handle the "worst" that could happen, the "best" that could happen and the "most likely" to happen.[1] Something to remember in reducing stress is to take time to plan your work and make the effort to work to your plan.

> By observing what entrepreneurs say and do, it is possible to understand their mental attitudes. Positive mental attitudes will greatly contribute to successful accomplishments. How entrepreneurs act is a reflection of what they think about themselves and their environment

HABITS AND ATTITUDES

Good habits are difficult to master, but once acquired they become important assets. Many top executives have acquired the habit of starting work in the early morning hours.

Getting up two or three hours earlier than usual might be one way of becoming more productive. This might require a great amount of effort, and be inconvenient. However, if the entrepreneur is able to follow this practice every day for a month, the activity will become a habit.

To use this early morning time productively, it would be helpful to decide the night before how it will be used. This will lead to another good habit: planning the next day's important activities before going to sleep each night.

If after the first month you want to retain your newly acquired habit, the chances are that it is a good one and that it will play an important part in your future performance.

When you understand that you are responsible for your actions, you should be willing to review your habits in relation to your future goals.

---

[1] See Milan Kubr (ed.): *Management consulting: A guide to the profession* (Geneva, ILO, 5th impr., 1980), Ch. 22.

New habits may have to be substituted for old habits, in order to help to prepare for future success.

Many people go through life wishing that they were someone else or that they were doing another type of work. Most people have a desire to change their life situation. But few people take action to do so.

A small proportion of people are willing to take risks to change their lives for the better. These people are entrepreneurial because they take advantage of opportunities to improve their lives. The true entrepreneur is the person who is constantly changing and growing. Having positive attitudes and a healthy self-image is essential for all entrepreneurs

LEADERSHIP

2

> The total performance of a business is mainly determined by the attitudes and actions of the entrepreneur. Your effectiveness as a leader is determined by the results you achieve

Successful entrepreneurs are successful leaders, whether they lead a few employees or a few hundred employees. By the very nature of their work, entrepreneurs are leaders because they must seek opportunities; initiate projects; gather the physical, financial and human resources needed to carry out projects; set goals for themselves and others; and direct and guide others to accomplish goals.

To be aware of better ways to accomplish tasks is to be an effective leader. You are likely to be a successful leader if you believe in continuous growth, improved efficiency and the continued success of your organisation.

DEVELOPING LEADERSHIP QUALITIES

Leadership qualities must be self-developed because these qualities vary with each person. Knowing that you are personally responsible for your leadership ability will help you to strive to make improvements. There is no one best way to become a leader. Entrepreneurs are individuals who have developed their own personal styles of leadership. If you try to pattern yourself slavishly after another leader, or some ideal set of characteristics, you never will be able to develop your own leadership talents and abilities to the fullest extent.

Your personality will help to influence your leadership behaviour. Your present job should provide a number of opportunities for you to practise leadership. Situations to improve your leadership ability can be found in your day-to-day activities and the interaction you have with your staff. Being aware of possibilities for demonstrating your leadership abilities in day-to-day activities is a good way to practise your skills. This testing of leadership ability will prepare you for more important leadership roles.

As a leader, you have the main responsibility for developing staff. Within the organisation, try to use your staff in the most effective manner. Because workers are the most important asset in an organisation, you must decide how each person's performance can be improved. Having done that, you can design opportunities for these workers to develop and improve their individual abilities. You should also evaluate workers' experiences to determine their success and the additional activities and responsibilities they might assume in the future.

The more of a leader you become, the more you will have to depend on your staff to support you and assume more of your responsibilities. Delegating responsibilities develops the trust and confidence that your staff need to achieve their full potential. As your employees achieve *their* potential, you will develop *your* potential as a leader.

To a great extent, leadership is an attitude which is demonstrated in the approach entrepreneurs have towards accomplishing tasks. A leader is usually willing to accept challenges which present great risks and great opportunities. A leader understands the total task to be accomplished and will often decide on new and innovative ways to accomplish it.

A guideline for good leadership is to "treat others as you would like to be treated". Trying to view a situation through the eyes of the other people involved will help in developing a "you" attitude. To determine your leadership qualities as an entrepreneur, you should be able to answer "yes" to the following questions:

- [ ] Are you a leader rather than a follower?
- [ ] Do people look to you for leadership and advice?
- [ ] Can you develop and implement new ideas?
- [ ] Do you take an active part in the life of the community?
- [ ] Do you continuously try to improve your strengths as well as eliminate your weaknesses?
- [ ] Do you organise your time and activities to be efficient?
- [ ] Do you have a specific plan or programme to improve your leadership capabilities?
- [ ] Do you allow other people to help you to achieve your goals?
- [ ] Do you learn from your mistakes?
- [ ] Are you result-oriented and do you finish something you start?

☐ Do you use your power as a leader to help others?

☐ Do other people have confidence in your abilities?

☐ Do the opinions of others help you to make your decisions?

☐ Are you able to deal with people effectively?

☐ Do you make changes in what you are doing to make your organisation better?

☐ Do you delegate authority and responsibility to your staff?

☐ Do you share your success with your staff?

Consider carefully each of these questions. Think of two occasions from your activities during the past two months when you exhibited a leadership quality.

> Increasing your leadership experience will result in the more efficient use of your time, better performance by your staff, and increased output. All these results can be measured

LEADERSHIP BEHAVIOUR

There are two main areas of leadership behaviour: (*a*) a goal-setting, planning, goal-achievement, *task-orientation*; and (*b*) a motivating, human relations, *person-orientation*.

Task-orientation

A leader with this orientation tends to exhibit the following behaviour patterns:

☐ clearly defines his own role and those of his staff;

☐ sets difficult but achievable goals and lets people know what is expected of them;

☐ sets procedures for measuring progress towards the goal and for measuring goal attainment, i.e. goals are clearly and specifically defined;

☐ actively exercises a leadership role in planning, directing, guiding and controlling goal-oriented activities;

☐ is interested in achieving productivity increases.

Leaders who score low on this orientation tend to be inactive in directing goal-orientated behaviour, such as planning or scheduling. They tend to work alongside their employees and do not clearly differentiate their role as the organisational leader.

Person-orientation

Persons who score high in this area of leadership behaviour tend to exhibit the following behaviour patterns:

☐ show concern for maintaining harmony in the organisation and easing tensions when they arise;

☐ show concern for workers as people rather than a means of production;

☐ show understanding and respect for employees' needs, goals, desires, feelings and *ideas*;

☐ establish good two-way communication with staff;

☐ apply the principle of reinforcement to improve worker performance (this principle states that those behaviours rewarded will increase in frequency, and those not rewarded (i.e. "punished") will decrease in frequency);

☐ delegate authority and responsibility, and encourage initiative;

☐ create an atmosphere of team work and co-operation in the organisation.

Leaders who score low on this orientation tend to be impersonal or cool in their relations with their employees, focus on individual performance and competition rather than co-operation, and do not delegate authority and responsibility.

Persons who rate high on person-orientation are not necessarily friendly, sociable people. Rather, they are able to deal effectively with different kinds of people. High person-orientation leaders show a high degree of skill in the area of human relations. In their relationships with their workers they tend to advise, co-ordinate, direct and initiate rather than criticise, disapprove and judge. They are persuasive rather than punitive. They exert strong influence and direction but in a manner which does not arouse resentment.

The characteristics common to high person-orientated leaders include the following:

☐ They understand their own needs, goals, values, limitations and capabilities. This understanding and knowledge of oneself is considered a necessary prerequisite for good relations with others.

☐ They are sensitive to the needs of others; they help people to fulfil these needs. By communicating with their employees, leaders can more effectively direct their efforts so that the company goals and employee needs are both being met.

☐ They appreciate and accept values and life-styles different from their own. They show an ability and a willingness to interact with persons quite different from themselves.

☐ They involve their employees in the company's goals by understanding their needs and by delegating authority and sharing responsibility.

☐ They possess good communication skills: they listen, ask questions, discuss and argue, and use the information they receive to direct and involve their workers in effective action.

> Although there is considerable variation in the leadership styles of entrepreneurs, the vast majority of entrepreneurs are high on task-orientation. Those entrepreneurs who have sustained success over long periods of time are also high on person-orientation

LEADING OTHERS

An important aspect of being a leader is the ability to achieve results by working with other people. You must be able to view situations through the eyes of the people you are leading. This is a humanistic approach to leadership because you are concerned with the feelings and attitudes of others, rather than being motivated just for personal reasons. It is through your actions that your leadership ability will be judged. If you respect your employees and treat them as an essential part of your business, they will probably treat you in a similar manner.

Some of your difficult problems, as a leader, will involve your employees. When faced with an employee problem, ask yourself: "How would I want to be treated if I were the employee?" Your response to this question will give you the information you need to make an appropriate decision. It is the implementation of this decision involving people that will determine the extent you consider your workers to be your organisation's most important asset.

Being concerned with the human aspects of work may be just as important as the wages and salaries that you pay your workers. If this is true, being a humanistic leader will cost you nothing in terms of money but may benefit you tremendously in terms of potential profits. Praise is one of the most important things you can give to workers, yet there is no cost involved. Freely giving praise to your workers can be a powerful incentive to increasing performance.

A leader is always concerned with making improvements which will benefit the organisation. By being creative and innovative, you demonstrate that you are interested in improving conditions within your organisation.

Your actions should reflect an innovative attitude to increasing your efficiency in whatever you do. Try to set high standards of performance for yourself. Most employees pattern their behaviour after their superiors, and it is important that everyone in an organisation who is in a leadership role should be performing at a high level. The higher up in an organisation a person is, the more that person must assume responsibility for personal actions and the actions of staff. You should work in the same enthusiastic manner as you want your staff to work. Your staff will probably assume the same work habits as you, so you must be sure to set a good example.

> To be an effective leader you must try to see things through the eyes of those you are leading. Before you take any action which affects your staff, consider how they will react to it. In your mind, you must be able to exchange places with your staff and think as they do

LEADING AND MOTIVATING OTHERS

Entrepreneurs are successful motivators of their employees. Some entrepreneurs motivate by the sheer example of their hard work, but entrepreneurs who are high on person-orientation tend to be the most successful motivators. The following are some methods that high person-orientated leaders would use to motivate staff.[1] How often do *you* use these techniques?

☐ *Build workers' self-esteem.* In general, the higher the workers' self-esteem, the better they perform in task-oriented situations. Therefore, build your employees' confidence in themselves by praising their good work and showing them that you expect their best efforts. Most people tend to live up to roles that are assigned to them.

☐ *Inform employees.* Try to tell your staff what you are trying to accomplish. Good communication within the organisation is essential to success. Few people are willing to give their best efforts unless they are aware of the purpose of their work. A good leader will explain to staff the reasons for doing particular activities. Your staff should not only know *what* work you are trying to accomplish but also understand *how* the work will be accomplished.

☐ *Delegate authority and responsibility.* Good leaders know how to delegate authority and responsibility. Your job is to achieve results, but you cannot do everything by yourself. As a leader, you must be able to trust others to accomplish your goals. Once your staff prove to

---

[1] See B. L. Rosenbaum: *Nation's Business* (Washington, DC, Chamber of Commerce of the United States), Mar. 1978.

18

be capable, they should have the freedom to make decisions, implement actions, make mistakes, take corrective action and achieve goals without constant supervision by you. If your employees are leaving for other jobs, this may indicate that you are not giving them the necessary opportunities to develop their talents. Every employee is a valuable asset to the organisation, and a leader must use these human assets to the fullest extent.

☐ *Maintain contact.* Use your leadership ability to maintain personal contact with your immediate colleagues. Be aware of their personality characteristics, abilities and potential capabilities. It is through personal contact that you will be able to use each person's talents most effectively.

☐ *Analyse the problem, not the person.* Avoid alluding to deficiencies in performance as indicators of a "poor attitude" or disinterest in the job. Focus instead on the problem. For example, your typist may be submitting uncorrected letters. Point out that the work must be checked before being presented to you, but avoid comments such as: "Why do you do this?" and "It shows you have no pride in your work." These comments lower a person's self-esteem and only add to the problem. Similarly, if your sales representative's calls are declining from, say, five per day to three per day, then focus on the problem itself. Don't say: "What have you been doing? Where's your drive? You used to be so enthusiastic!" but rather: "You must increase your daily calls from three to five. Now let's see how we can do this." Of course, there are times when you may have to probe beneath the surface. For example, a sales representative may be suffering from ill-health or may have domestic problems. In these cases you should actively listen and show a genuine interest in your employee's feelings and needs. It is especially important to maintain the workers' self-esteem, and not add to their problems.

☐ *Apply the reinforcement principle.* You should reward behaviour that you consider desirable, because people tend to repeat rewarded behaviour. Do not reward behaviour that you consider undesirable, because people tend not to repeat behaviour that is unrewarded.

Other points to note about the reinforcement principle are:

—— You can never give too much positive reinforcement: that is, continually reward desirable behaviour whether this involves a minor act (such as your secretary working a few minutes overtime to type an important letter), or something major (such as your secretary suggesting a new, more efficient filing system).

—— Reward is most effective when applied immediately following the desirable behaviour. If you hear that the marketing manager has achieved record sales, call and congratulate the marketing staff that same day.

—— Be sure that the rewards are seen as such by your employees. What might be a major reward for one person may be minor to another. An obvious example is that a $100 bonus to an employee earning $7,500 a year would be far more rewarding than the same amount to an employee earning $17,500 a year. Similarly, some employees would consider a public statement within the company about their achievement to be a sufficient reward, whereas others would require something more tangible such as financial reward or improvement in status.

—— Apply more reward at the outset of a desired behaviour change than after the behaviour pattern is established.

☐ *Be an active listener.* Active listening requires that you explicitly give feedback to people speaking to you. In emotional exchanges it is important that you feedback not only the content of what has been said but also the feeling or attitude that was expressed at the time. For example, a quality control supervisor might complain: "You expect my people to detect *all* the defective components that come through. But we've only got three people down there and at the rate those components are coming through, it's almost impossible. You ought to come down and try it yourself some time." Practise active listening by replying as follows: "You think that your present manpower is insufficient to handle the current production rate, and that we expect too much work from them. You also feel that we're out of touch with the situation down there." At this point you are simply ensuring that the supervisor knows that you understand the complaint; you do not offer any opinion of your own. Once the supervisor knows that his complaint is understood, the lines of communication are open for you to discuss a solution to the problem.

☐ *Set specific goals and continually review them.* Set specific, clearly understood, measurable goals. Make sure those concerned understand the goals and that you believe they are capable of achieving them (i.e. build self-esteem). These goals should be difficult but achievable. Goals that are too easy or too difficult do not motivate people. Achievable goals, when achieved, build self-confidence. Setting specific dates for reviewing progress toward goals maintains motivation by requiring people to make reportable progress by these dates.

☐ *Take corrective action.* When you must deal with some negative aspect of a worker's performance, you should talk to that worker in private. Never criticise a worker in public. If workers are doing something wrong, you must take corrective action, but it should be taken in a way that does not hurt their feelings or embarrass them.

Even though your employees may occasionally make mistakes, they probably perform most of their duties in an effective manner. You should give credit to them for the many things they do well before you react negatively to a specific aspect of their work. After you highlight those things that they perform well, you should indicate those aspects of their job which they might improve. Because every discussion with workers should end on a positive note, you should remind them of the importance of their specific contributions to the efficient running of the business. Tell them that you appreciate all the good work that they have done.

As a general principle of good leadership, the more interest you show in your workers, the harder they will work for you. There are as many leadership styles as there are leaders. However, if you truly put the interests of your workers first, the probability of your success will increase. Being human in your relationships with your employees will almost certainly result in greater efficiency and larger profits

---

ACTION LEADERSHIP

Most leaders have the ability to take action and achieve results. Although you "make progress slowly", you should try to achieve specific goals each day. The following suggestions may be helpful to you in increasing your leadership ability:

☐ Once you have made a decision, take action as soon as possible.

☐ Your efforts can be multiplied through the talents and abilities of your staff. To be a good leader you should know how and when to use these abilities by having capable people around you who support you and who believe in you as a leader.

☐ You will gain confidence in your leadership abilities if you concentrate on developing your strengths. Avoid situations which would reveal your weaknesses.

☐ A good leader is willing to admit mistakes and revise plans. You must realise that conditions change continually and adjustments must be made from time to time.

The longer you have been in your current job, the more probable it is that you have developed specific habits and a set routine. You may be surprised at the number of unproductive things you are doing. Write down all the possible ways you might increase your personal efficiency during the next two weeks. By eliminating these unproductive (but time-consuming) activities, you will create time for more leadership-related activities. Some time-consuming activities cannot be eliminated, but these should be delegated to your secretary or others as far as possible.

Most leaders are active people who are engaged in a variety of productive activities and are able to achieve good results. Whenever possible, you should be able to identify the results of your activities in terms of real, tangible and visible outcomes. It is important for you to know exactly what you hope to accomplish in each activity. Identifying what you want to accomplish in terms of objectives will provide direction for your actions. These objectives can be written for a day (as shown below), a week, a month or year. As an active leader, you will be judged on what you do and how well you do it. Thus:

Objectives for today

1. I will complete the planning section of the report.
2. I will determine the safety needs of the manufacturing department by visiting that department and talking to five shop-floor workers, two supervisors, the trade union representative and the department manager.
3. I will review the personnel budget and make necessary changes.

> If you know exactly what you want to accomplish, the more likely it is that you will take action which leads to success. Your attitude towards work will affect your accomplishments

IMPROVE EMPLOYEE MORALE

Choose compatible people to work in your business. A true test of leadership is the ability to bring together persons having different abilities and personalities to work together towards common goals. Positive job attitudes depend to a large extent on the ability of individuals to do their jobs competently. It is your responsibility to develop worker attitudes and it is up to you to apply the leadership necessary to ensure that these attitudes are positive. Questions regarding the use of your leadership ability to improve employee morale include:

☐ Are your employees satisfied with their working conditions?

☐ Do all employees know their individual roles in the organisation; and do they know how these roles contribute to the total operation of the organisation?

☐ Do you correct unsafe working conditions which may create negative employee attitudes?

☐ How have you demonstrated your concern for the health and welfare of your employees?

☐ How do you measure the morale of your personnel?

☐ In what specific ways do you try to improve the morale of your personnel?

☐ Do you take a positive approach in maintaining a unified and cohesive organisation?

☐ How do your training programmes accommodate individual workers' needs?

☐ How do you evaluate the performance of each individual worker?

☐ Are your staff able to implement their ideas?

☐ Do you acknowledge and give credit to your staff for their contributions to the over-all goals of the organisation?

☐ Do you allow people to solve their work-related problems?

These and other questions will help you to identify areas where you can use your leadership ability to improve the working conditions of employees.

> Entrepreneurs are leaders by the very nature of their activities. Effective person-oriented leaders are highly skilled in motivating and communicating with their employees. They understand their employees' needs and endeavour to involve their employees in accomplishing company objectives

RISK-TAKING

3

> Entrepreneurs are calculated risk-takers. They enjoy the excitement of a challenge, but they don't gamble. Entrepreneurs avoid low-risk situations because there is a lack of challenge and avoid high-risk situations because they want to succeed. They like *achievable* challenges

Entrepreneurs like to take realistic risks because they want to be successful: that is, they take great satisfaction in accomplishing difficult but realistic tasks by applying their own skills. Hence, low-risk situations and high-risk situations are avoided because this source of satisfaction is unlikely in either case. In short, the entrepreneur likes a difficult but achievable challenge.

As the size of your business expands, your problems and opportunities become more numerous and complex. Business growth and development require that you are not afraid to make decisions and are willing to assume certain risks. Most people are afraid to take risks because they want to be safe and avoid failure. However, all phases of your work involve risk-taking, which is an essential part of being an entrepreneur. You have to work under the pressures and conditions of risk-taking and should understand that the possibility of failure is always present.

WHAT IS A RISK SITUATION?

A risk situation occurs when you are required to make a choice between two or more alternatives whose potential outcomes are not known and must be subjectively evaluated. A risk situation involves potential success and potential loss. The greater the possible loss, the greater the risk involved.

As a risk-taker, you will have to make decisions in conditions of uncertainty, balancing potential success against potential loss. Whether or not you choose a "risky" alternative or a "conservative" alternative depends on: (a) the attractiveness of each alternative; (b) the extent to which you are prepared to accept the potential loss; (c) the relative probabilities of success and failure; and (d) the degree to which your own efforts increase the likelihood of success and decrease the likelihood of failure.

For example, you may have a secure job, earning $10,000 a year, with promotion probable every five years or so. You may have the opportunity to buy a company whose future is uncertain but whose current owner's salary is $20,000 a year. The company may continue to be very successful or it may fail in one or two years. Your choice is between staying in a secure position with moderate, predictable financial and career rewards, or taking a risk and possibly achieving very high financial and career rewards.

Some people would not think of taking such a risk, regardless of the probabilities of success. They prefer to stay in secure positions. Others are impetuous, dissatisfied with their present position, and looking for the "magic pot of gold" or some amazing streak of luck to make them rich. These people tend to be influenced by the size of the potential reward offered. They pay little regard to the probability of success, and do not give much thought to the degree of effort required on their part. Attracted by hopes of high return with little effort, they are pure gamblers.

The entrepreneur's assessment of the situation is very different from that of both the above types of people, although the entrepreneur shares certain characteristics with them. The essential difference is that an entrepreneur will systematically and thoroughly assess the likelihood of the company's success and the extent to which his efforts could influence this likelihood. If the entrepreneur is able to have a considerable influence on whether or not the company is successful, he is very likely to make the purchase.

Another essential element in the entrepreneur's approach to risk-taking situations is the willingness to accept personal responsibility for the consequences of the decision, regardless of whether the consequences are favourable or unfavourable. Other persons find it difficult to accept personal responsibility for decisions which may lead to failure, and they often attribute events in their lives to luck or to forces beyond their control, such as competition with big business or government interference. These people either go for the hundred-to-one shots, and cross their fingers, or fatalistically reject all risk situations because they believe that they have no influence at all on the outcomes.

Most entrepreneurial traits are inter-related. This is particularly so with risk-taking behaviour. Here are several inter-relations:

☐ Risk-taking is related to creativity and innovation, and it is an essential part in turning ideas into reality.

☐ Risk-taking is related to self-confidence. The more confidence you have in your own abilities, the greater confidence you will have in being able to affect the outcome of your decisions and a greater willingness to take what others see as risks.

☐ Realistic knowledge of your own capabilities is also important. Such realism serves to restrict your activities to situations in which you *can* affect the outcomes.

However, not all your risk-taking behaviour is as cold and objective as the above implies. There is also the entrepreneurial excitement regarding uncertainty, and the drive and enthusiasm to ensure that the consequences are successful.

PERSONAL RISK-TAKING

Risk-taking is essential to realising your own potential as an entrepreneur. Experiences in risk-taking in personal relations with spouse, friends and neighbours will help you to gain experience in judging the odds, risking what is necessary, and avoiding risks which have little potential reward.

Risk-taking in your personal life involves an awareness of past events; a concern for the future; and a desire to live in the present. If you are unwilling to take risks, you will never realise your potential for self-fulfilment and self-realisation. Your personal and professional growth come from living in the present and taking the necessary risks to achieve your goals in the future.

As an entrepreneur, you should realise that growth comes from taking advantage of present opportunities in your personal as well as your business life, and taking risks to achieve goals. Some of the most important risks are those in which you learn something new about yourself. Situations which involve personal risks should challenge your abilities and capacities to the fullest extent. Don't underestimate your own worth, because you are probably capable of achieving much more than you actually do. Risk-taking is an important part of personal growth; it is also useful in conducting your business activities.

Taking personal responsibility for your own actions decreases your dependence on others. Entrepreneurs are responsible people because they have the strength and ability to determine their own future. When other people are responsible for your actions, it means that you have less control over your own future. The result of not taking total responsibility for your own personal actions is that you are not able to live life to the full. As soon as you know something is wrong in your life, then is the time to assume responsibility for correcting it. Otherwise the situation only becomes worse as time passes, and the problem will become more difficult to solve.

There is no risk until you assume control for your own decisions and are willing to stand by your actions. Risk is not involved in decisions where there is no possibility of loss. Most decisions concerning your own life involve some risk and it is for those decisions that you are fully responsible. Knowing you are solely responsible will help you to make decisions more confidently, which in turn will minimise the risk.

It may be difficult to separate personal and business goals because your business is very much a part of your life. You should not risk more than you can afford to lose. This is a warning that you should observe because from time to time you may be tempted to risk everything on one idea.

As an entrepreneur, you should not take unnecessary risks. You must have control over your emotions and accept risk only when the benefits are equal to or greater than the risk involved. Your first task must be to decide whether the goal is important enough to justify the risk.

In some instances, you will have to use your intuition in evaluating any course of action which involves risk. Your intuition will help to determine the extent of the risk and the possible outcomes. The most intangible, yet some of the most important, factors in determining risk are your own talents, abilities and past experiences.

> You are responsible for everything in your life, including your successes and failures. However, success will be easier to achieve if you are willing and able to take the necessary calculated risks

DEVELOPING CREATIVE IDEAS

Risk-taking and creativity are two essential characteristics of entrepreneurs. By trying to be more creative, you will also become aware of more productive ideas. When you are able to choose from a number of good ideas, you will be more willing to take the necessary risks to implement your most productive idea.

To some degree, everyone is *creative*. Under most circumstances, it is possible to develop a person's creative talents. When you have developed a creative idea, certain risks may be involved in having the idea implemented. To reduce the risks of having an idea rejected, the following suggestions may be helpful:

- ☐ Try to explain your idea to your spouse or friend. It is often better to talk about an idea before writing it down. Explaining an idea will lead to discussion, which might result in modification. Only when the idea has become firm should it be written down. Even then it is likely to change many times before it is in its final form.

- ☐ Choose the time and place to present your idea to others. Don't present a new idea to your organisation during a crisis. The organisation should have a certain amount of stability before any new ideas are introduced. Timing is extremely important to the presentation of a new idea. Try to choose a time when others will be most receptive to something new.

- ☐ Present your idea a little at a time. First, present the over-all concept. Present details as time passes and as others become interested in your idea.

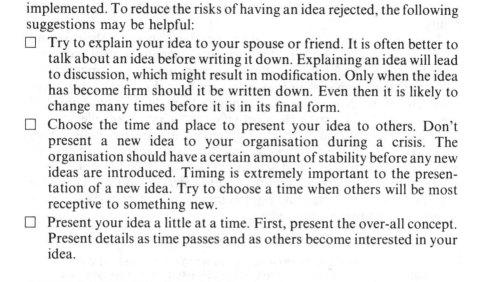

> Never force your idea on others. People need time to accept anything new. An idea which may involve the future of an organisation involves risk. Whenever there is risk, people are hesitant and are likely to have many doubts

TYPES OF RISK-TAKERS

The type of risk-taker you are depends to some degree on the extent to which you are influenced by other people, your past experiences, your present situation and your expectations for the future. Within a business there is a need to have risk-takers of various types.

At the lower levels of your organisation there is a need to have workers who are good at doing routine things where little risk is involved. Most of your workers should be risk-takers of this type because their behaviour will be predictable and will bring organisational stability.

At the middle management level there is more room for risk-taking. Middle managers should have some freedom to be innovative and make minor modifications in procedures and functions. These persons may be considered risk-takers, but their impact on the total organisation should be minimal.

Entrepreneurs, at the top of the organisation structure, have the capacity to formulate and implement creative ideas. To be successful in business, entrepreneurs must take risks to make their ideas become reality.

Some entrepreneurs may be called "practical" because their organisations grow only to the extent that they can personally control and direct the various aspects of them. Practical entrepreneurs are goal-oriented and are confident enough of their ideas to accept the risks to make their ideas work. However, they are practical enough to realise the limitations of their ideas and will restrict their activities to "what is possible".

Highly creative and innovative entrepreneurs are moderately high risk-takers, willing to accept change, try various alternatives and develop innovations for products and services in new areas of business. These highly innovative entrepreneurs are usually leaders in business. They have ideas and are able to find the right combinations of people and other resources to implement their ideas.

> As an entrepreneur, you must be a planner in the sense that you can visualise how your creative ideas might be used. However, you must also have the risk-taking ability to be able to implement your ideas and carry them to successful conclusions

DELEGATION OF AUTHORITY AND RESPONSIBILITY

As an entrepreneur, you are a leader in the sense that you direct the activities of others to help to achieve organisational goals. As an individual, you can achieve only so much before you need the help of others to achieve the higher-level goals of your organisation. As the leader of an organisation composed of people, you must be willing to give authority and responsibility for certain activities to your staff.

Delegating authority and responsibility to others involves certain risks. It may have positive or negative effects, and you will have to live with the results. If you are a growth-oriented entrepreneur, you *must* have staff who are action-oriented and capable of assuming authority and responsibility.

To obtain maximum benefits, your employees must have a certain degree of power and freedom to carry out their duties and responsibilities. As an entrepreneur, you need help from other people; however, you probably don't have time to monitor their work closely. The extent to which you trust and have faith in your staff will be indicated by your responses to the questions listed in the Rating Chart in figure 2. The responses to these questions will give some indication of your willingness

Figure 2. Rating Chart

To what extent do you:	Ratings (tick one response)			
	Not at all	Sometimes	Frequently	Extensively
☐ Allow staff freedom to express their ideas and abilities?				
☐ Permit staff to take risks for activities for which they are completely responsible?				
☐ Delegate authority?				
☐ Risk not closely watching and controlling your staff?				
☐ Believe that staff can produce good results on their own if they are given the opportunity?				
☐ Risk delegating to find out who are most able to accept authority and responsibility?				

to risk delegating authority and responsibility to people in your organisation. It is only when you are able to delegate activities to others that you can devote more time to higher-level activities such as long-range planning or the development of new products.

> Risk-taking is especially important in delegating authority and responsibility to your staff. Allowing others to share your power is a characteristic of growth-oriented entrepreneurs. The more you can delegate power successfully, the more time you will have to deal with those activities having the greatest impact on your organisation's future success

IMPLEMENTING CHANGE

In any activity you must first determine whether or not a risk is involved. In a risk situation, your power, position or authority may be challenged. When you know something is wrong in your business, you should be able to appraise the situation realistically and try to solve the problem. You must be ready to take the necessary corrective action, which will probably involve some risk.

When a risk situation is apparent to you, the decision to risk or not becomes very important. When you decide to risk, you should follow a definite plan for initiating action. Alternative plans may also be devised in case the first plan does not succeed. These alternatives allow flexibility in case the conditions of the problem change.

Once a plan of action is devised, it must be activated. It is only when the plan is initiated that you can really know and understand the risks that are involved. At first, you may receive little feedback regarding your decision. This lack of feedback may create doubts in your mind. It is during the early stages after the decision has been implemented that you must be fully committed to your decision until the problem has been solved. The conviction with which you attack the problem is critical. When you are convinced that a certain course of action will solve the problem, your specific actions will help to determine the outcome. Promoting your decision and gaining the support of others will help to make the decision successful.

The risk-taking ability of entrepreneurs is enhanced by:

☐ their self-confidence;

☐ their willingness to use their capacities to the fullest extent to move the odds in their favour;

☐ their capacity to assess realistically the risk situation and their ability to alter the odds; and

☐ looking at the risk situation in terms of their established goals.

The act of risk-taking is an essential part of being an entrepreneur. You must set high goals for yourself, and then use all your abilities and talents to achieve these goals. The higher the goals, the greater the risks involved.

Innovations in business which result in higher-quality goods and services are the result of action by entrepreneurs who are willing to accept great challenges and take calculated risks

---

EVALUATING YOUR RISK

Quantitative data (numbers) will help you to evaluate any risk, as well as establish your goals and make it possible for you to chart, systematically, your progress. Finally, through quantitative data you will be able to measure the results achieved in relation to your original objectives.

You should know that the numbers are accurate and what they represent. These quantitative data will support your own knowledge, background and experience in making decisions.

Evaluate your own needs before you decide to take a risk. Some of the questions you should ask before making any decision involving risk include:

☐ Is the goal worth the risk involved?

☐ How can the risk be minimised?

☐ What information is needed before taking the risk?

☐ What people and other resources can help to minimise the risk and achieve this goal?

☐ Why is this risk important?

☐ What fears do you have in taking this risk?

☐ Are you willing to try your best to achieve the goal?

☐ What will be achieved by taking this risk?

☐ What preparation do you need to make before you take the risk?

☐ How will you know (in quantitative terms) when you have accomplished your goal?

☐ What are the biggest obstacles in achieving your goal?

This questioning procedure is essential to the risk-taking process. The questions listed are merely examples of the many you must ask before entering into a risk situation. Taking a risk before answering these questions will probably lead to failure.

In business, as in life, there is clearly no way to avoid risk-taking. When you take risks, you discover your own abilities; and you become better able to control your own future. You become more self-assured, and have a more positive outlook towards risk-taking because you have faith in your own abilities; you accept risks as challenges which require your best efforts to achieve goals

---

EXAMPLE OF RISK-TAKING

Entrepreneurial risk-taking behaviour is being more and more recognised as important for top-level management. Many companies now are choosing risk-taking, innovating, entrepreneurial men and women, rather than maintenance management, when the company's situation requires a growth strategy.

Although risk-taking is a style of behaviour, calculated risk-taking is a skill that can be improved. Here are suggested procedures for analysing a risk situation.

Assess the risk

The first step is to establish whether or not a risk is involved: that is, whether there is a potential loss involved in choosing one particular alternative. For example, you may be faced with the need for increased production to meet increased demand. Your choices are to:

☐ stay with your current level of demand;

☐ purchase more equipment to meet the demand;

☐ lease more equipment to meet the demand; or

☐ subcontract production to smaller manufacturers.

If your business has a good cash flow, strong cash reserves or good credit facilities, and if demand is certain to grow in the foreseeable future, there is little risk involved in deciding on any of the alternatives—although the first alternative would be a foolish option to take up because it ignores the opportunity for profit growth.

On the other hand, continued demand may not be assured. For example, your product or service may become obsolete because of competitive innovations; more companies may enter the field; or the market may be nearing saturation. Furthermore, your business may not be able to afford an investment of the amount required without a guaranteed return on it. In this situation there is clearly a risk involved in deciding whether to expand production. However, there are clearly different *degrees* of risk—and corresponding different degrees of potential return (success)—for the different alternatives. How can you assess the alternatives?

Goals and objectives

Your next step would be to consider your company's policies and objectives. A company objective might be to achieve slow growth, or steady growth, or non-growth, or growth in other product areas. *You* must decide whether the risk involved is consistent with your objectives. If it is, the decision-making process continues; and a detailed assessment of the alternatives is undertaken.

Clarify the alternatives

Given that some degree of risk-taking (i.e. a decision to expand production) is consistent with your company's objectives, the next step is to survey the various alternatives. These alternatives should be specified in sufficient detail so that the costs involved can be assessed objectively. Most costs will be financial costs, but you should always include personal, social and physical costs when appropriate. For example, will an alternative require excessive personal effort? Will failure lead to a loss in social prestige? You need to specify the financial and other costs for each of the viable alternatives.

Gather information and weigh the alternatives

The next stage is one of intensive information-gathering so that a realistic assessment of the odds can be made for each alternative. Market estimates would be made for demand under various predicted conditions. The likelihood of competitive reactions would be assessed and the effects of these reactions calculated. Various consequences should be followed through to their logical conclusions:

- ☐ If demand nears saturation point, can product modification stimulate increased demand in new markets?
- ☐ Are new markets available if competitive activity decreases current market share?
- ☐ Can the machinery be easily modified to handle other products?
- ☐ Are suppliers and subcontractors likely to increase their charges if demand grows?

The likely return to your company for each alternative should be assessed on the basis of market information, forecasts of future demand, assessments of competitive reactions, and various other predictions— including the behaviour of those involved in the situation, such as finance companies or equipment manufacturers.

How can risks be minimised?

This crucial step involves a realistic assessment of the extent to which you can affect the odds. It involves:

- ☐ a clear awareness of your abilities and the company's capacities;

☐ some creativity in determining how the odds may be changed (increased in your favour);

☐ the ability to plan strategy and tactics to effect the change; and

☐ the drive, energy and enthusiasm to implement the strategy.

Plan and implement an alternative

Once an alternative is selected, a plan is then drawn up for its implementation. This would include a time-table, a clear definition of the goal, a set of contingency plans for possible outcomes, and a feedback process so that necessary changes can be implemented quickly.

DECISION-MAKING

4

To be entrepreneurial, you must be creative, especially when it comes to decision-making. You must strongly believe in yourself and your ability to make good decisions. It is this decision-making ability that is the distinguishing mark of an entrepreneur

---

It is you who will make the decisions having the greatest impact on the future of your organisation. In many cases, the more important the decision you have to make, the less relevant information will be available. Quantitative data are usually available for making routine decisions; but these facts and numbers are likely to be less important when making top-level decisions affecting the organisation's future.

In large organisations senior management usually base their decisions on firm data and documentation contained in surveys, reports and committee recommendations. This information has usually been gathered in a standardised manner, in accordance with techniques used in solving problems. It is possible for a major problem to be split up so that a part of it can be solved immediately—generally to meet an urgent need where the results are fairly certain. A decision is usually reached by an established procedure well understood by management; and it may represent a consensus, many individuals being unwilling to accept personal responsibility for the decision in question.

You, as an entrepreneur, will have to be more creative than conventional managers, partly because you will have to make decisions without the assistance of quantitative data or experienced support staff. You may have to look at a problem from different angles and seek an innovative way in which to solve it.

You must speculate by relying on your own hunches and ideas. When being unconventional, you must always take full responsibility for your actions. Put every problem in its broader context, taking into account that major decisions will have long-term effects on your total business operation.

Success as an entrepreneur depends on your ability to make decisions which improve the future profitability of your business. Intuitive decision-making ability, a most valuable entrepreneurial resource, comes from years of experience of being exposed to making necessary decisions in increasingly complex situations.

The more your environment changes, the more judgements and intuitive decisions you will have to make. Mistakes will occur, but you must be quick to recognise them and take corrective action. Quantitative data can support your judgement, but will not replace the intuition underlying many of your more entrepreneurial decisions.

A decision can be good or bad according to how it is implemented. In some situations your insight will enable you to visualise the results of a certain course of action. In others, if you think you might be too emotionally involved, you should deliberately seek to identify weaknesses in the plan. In doing so, you will become more objective.

Use past experiences as guidelines in arriving at decisions, but remember that no two decision-making situations are exactly the same. Although problems may be similar, situational and external factors affecting them will differ

---

BEING A CAPABLE DECISION-MAKER

The more experienced you are in decision-making, the more you will be self-confident and action-oriented. Answers to the following questions may be helpful in determining your present capacity for decision-making:

☐ How do you maintain self-confidence when making an important decision?

☐ What examples from the past six months illustrate your ability to make realistic decisions?

☐ What fears or weaknesses do you have when making decisions?

☐ In what ways do you use creativity and/or intuition when making decisions?

☐ What have you learned from mistakes you made in previous decisions?

☐ In what ways do you procrastinate and delay making decisions?

☐ Do you give up or avoid problems which appear difficult?

☐ How well do you adjust to changes which occur around you?

☐ Are you usually forced into making decisions?

☐ What action do you take once you have reached a decision?

☐ How do you provide the leadership necessary to achieve the desired outcomes?

☐ How do you use resources in your environment to make decisions?

☐ In what ways do you use your personal and professional contacts to gain information which will help you to make a decision?

If you are capable of making decisions within reasonable time-limits, you are probably capable of taking advantage of business opportunities as they appear. Sometimes you have to make a quick decision to make the most of an opportunity.

Problem-solving

Great attention has been given to rational aspects of decision-making. The "scientific method" of problem-solving indicates that there are specific procedures to follow in order to solve a problem and make a decision. These usually involve the following steps:

☐ become acquainted with the problem in general;

☐ determine the key facts relating to it;

☐ identify major problem(s);

☐ identify related problems;

☐ search for possible causes of the problem;

☐ consider potential solutions to the problem;

☐ select the most feasible solution;

☐ implement the solution; and

☐ verify that the solution is correct.

This rational approach is a logical and sensible way to solve most business problems. However, the "scientific method" will not guarantee that a particular solution will work; your leadership and power are needed to implement a solution successfully.

Problem-solving and implementing solutions are not difficult when you are working in an environment with which you are familiar. Decisions can usually be made quickly and accurately because they are based on your previous experiences.

To be effective, you must be able to see every aspect of a problem, as well as understand it in its entirety. Most people in your organisation, involved in specific and limited activities, can see parts of the problem; but it is up to you to put *all* the parts together so that a complete grasp of it becomes possible.

Your past experience and intuition will enable you to pick out the vital factors and issues in any problem. From these, you will be alert to significant differences between *how it is* and *how it ought to be*.

> Key problems in any organisation are those where there is little or no past experience to use for guidance. When the problem environment is new and unfamiliar, a different orientation is required. To be entrepreneurial, you must be able to solve problems on unfamiliar ground

Making decisions

Many key problems can be solved in different ways. When facts alone are not enough to form a basis to select one course of action, decisions are made under a high degree of uncertainty where the risks may not be known. Guidelines for making key decisions include the following:

☐ Determine those facts of the problem with which you are familiar. Try not to mix facts and opinions.

☐ Identify those areas of the problem which are not based on facts. These unknown areas are where you must use reasoning, logic and intuition to arrive at a decision.

☐ Avoid making a key decision which will drastically change the present form of your organisation. Decisions of this type should be worked out over a period of time.

☐ Take moderate risks when there is a high degree of uncertainty.

☐ Implement decisions on a "trial" basis. This reduces your risks and allows you to observe the results before becoming fully committed to a decision.

☐ In some circumstances, it might be better for you to continue to do what has worked successfully in the past. Using untried methods and experimenting with new ideas could lead to disaster.

☐ Even though a decision may not be the best possible, it might lead to highly successful results. Be willing to take aggressive action to implement a decision. The extent to which your power and force are behind a decision will affect the results.

Boldness and enthusiasm are required in implementing a decision. Be positive about the future outcomes of a decision. Don't spend time hesitating. Once you begin implementing a decision, all doubts and uncertainties should be left behind.

As an entrepreneur, you must be decisive in your actions. your organisation should have definite purposes and clearly identified goals to achieve. Most entrepreneurs have little fear of decision-making because they do not expect to fail. They set their own standards for success.

You should have a sense of security from knowing that you are in command of your future. This feeling of security allows you to make key decisions with little fear of the consequences. This sense of security also allows you to enter new areas of business; the entrepreneur leads and others follow.

> Dealing with ambiguity and uncertainty are important characteristics of entrepreneurs. You should have a positive attitude toward decision-making. This positive attitude will help you to use decision-making as a positive force in attaining the goals and aspirations of your organisation

DETERMINING SOLUTIONS

Once a problem has been defined and all relevant information and data have been collected, you must identify possible solutions to the problem. You may want to begin with a "brainstorming" session where a group of people discuss with each other and develop a list of possible alternative solutions.

This brainstorming technique often results in unique contributions by the participants, since they see the problem from various viewpoints. Never criticise or reject any solution suggested during the brainstorming session. It is important that you encourage group members to develop as many potential solutions as possible. If necessary, give hints and suggestions to keep the discussion active, and encourage additional comments and ideas from the participants.

The following criteria may prove useful when you evaluate a proposed solution:

☐ Is the solution logical?
☐ Is it possible to put the solution into practice?
☐ What additional problems are created by the solution?

When the group reviews all possible solutions on the list, some solutions may be combined while other solutions may be eliminated. When the group has reduced the options to three or four, you may want to consider each potential solution extensively and in depth. Although many problems have no single *right* solution, it is up to you to determine the best possible solution to meet your needs.

Figure 3.   Problem-Solving Chart [1]

	Alternative solutions	Potential advantages	Potential disadvantages	Potential consequences
(1)				
(2)				
(3)				
(4)				

[1]   Do not try to write too much on this chart. It is meant to be a guide when you are starting out, by providing a system to identify positive and negative features of your problems.

The Problem-Solving Chart shown in figure 3 is one way of organising possible solutions to problems. After completing it you will be able to analyse alternative solutions in terms of potential advantages, disadvantages and consequences.

Space is provided in the chart for a maximum of four possible solutions. If there are more than four possible solutions, it may be difficult for you to analyse the information adequately. Listing potential advantages will indicate how each potential solution will benefit you. The potential disadvantages will illustrate how the potential solution will adversely affect you. In some instances, an advantage or disadvantage may be the same for two or more alternative solutions.

The potential consequences identified in the last column will be the results of analysing the potential advantages and disadvantages. They should equal the potential net result of implementing a particular solution. The Problem-Solving Chart can help entrepreneurs to analyse and solve major problems which would otherwise have an adverse effect on the business.

Another procedure for analysing potential solutions in the Problem-Solving Chart is to identify reasons "for" and reasons "against" each potential solution. The form shown in figure 4 can be used to evaluate each potential solution.

To use the Solution Evaluation Form to the best advantage, you should:

☐ Write a brief description of the problem at the top of the form.

☐ Write a brief description of the proposed solution.

☐ In the "Reasons for" column, list important factors which would favour implementing the proposed solution.

☐ In the "Reasons against" column, list important factors for not implementing the proposed solution.

☐ *Rate* each factor by its importance to you. The numerical rating might be 1, 2, 3, 4, 5, where a low rating of 1 indicates that the factor affects the problem only slightly and a high rating of 5 indicates that the factor is extremely important in making your decision. Each factor in the "Reasons for" column and each factor in the "Reasons against" column would receive a numerical rating.

☐ Add the ratings in each of the two "Numerical ratings" columns. The column with the higher total will give you some indication of the potential for a particular solution. If there is a big difference between the two totals (in favour of "Reasons for" the solution), you may feel more secure in the use of this technique to make a decision. If there is little difference in totals for both columns, it might indicate that you need additional information about the problem.

43

Figure 4. Solution Evaluation Form

Problem description:			
Problem solution:			
Numerical rating	Reasons for	Reasons against	Numerical rating

☐ Use the Solution Evaluation Form for the top two or three solutions identified in the Problem-Solving Chart. Comparing the results should help to make your decision easier.

> Forms can help you to organise information logically and systematically in order to assist you in the decision-making process

IMPLEMENTING DECISIONS

The entrepreneur's personality and his attitude toward implementing a decision affect the eventual outcome. Once a decision has been made, you should not hesitate to implement it. People respect those who are action-oriented and are willing to stand by their decisions.

Try to surround yourself with key people who are willing to accept your decisions and take the necessary actions to implement them quickly. If staff continually doubt your decisions, you too will begin to have doubts. These doubts can lead to unnecessary delays and insecurity on your part and on the part of others in your organisation.

If possible, don't fully commit yourself to one solution before trying it out in a small way. When a decision has been made to solve a problem in a particular manner, it may be necessary to alter the procedures for implementation. As time passes, and as the solution is being implemented, new facts and circumstances may appear which alter the original situation.

Some decisions you make can be changed; others cannot. It is fortunate that most decisions *can* be changed—if action to do so is taken in time. Once you understand that most decisions *can* be changed, you will have more confidence in your decision-making abilities.

You will have more control over your decisions than most people if you follow the principle that "most decisions can be changed". You can practise decision-making by taking small risks when making decisions to move in a new direction or towards a new goal. It is much easier to make these decisions if you can see that your decisions can be changed. You must learn to distinguish between decisions you can change and those you cannot change. Before making a decision you should ask the question: "If I fail to achieve the desired results, to what extent can I reverse my decision?"

Decisions which can be changed can be implemented quickly. If others are affected by the decision, it would be wise to inform them that the decision may be changed if specific results are not achieved. Staff who are expected to implement your decision are more likely to assume responsibility for the decision when they know that if the expected change is not achieved they will not be blamed. There seems to be a direct relationship between the action orientation of an organisation and the way in which staff treat decisions which are reversible.

Timing is extremely important in decision-making, especially when a business is expanding. In some instances decisions must be made quickly and implemented immediately. Some entrepreneurial decisions are made without knowledge of future conditions, developments or changing conditions. Effective monitoring of the implementation of your decision will reveal any weaknesses in it—and will provide information for future decision-making.

Critical decisions are not easy to make and they may be required frequently. The one thing worse than making a wrong decision is avoiding making any decision. Remember that decision-making is an art; the more you practise it, the more expert you will become

---

BUSINESS PLANNING

5

> Planning helps to establish company goals. As your company grows, the greater need there is for planning; you begin to spend more time planning and less time doing routine operating activities

In most businesses there are two kinds of planning activities. First, there are the entrepreneurial activities, including such tasks as making contacts with bankers, accountants, lawyers, and others who help with the financial and legal aspects of your business. Obtaining marketing surveys, conducting product research and designing budgets are all entrepreneurial aspects of business planning. Second, there are those aspects of the business which may be considered routine. These include preparing monthly financial reports, monitoring and revising budgets, managing the flow of production and marketing products and services.

You can hire managers and supervisors to do the routine activities; but *you* must be deeply involved with the entrepreneurial aspects of your business. It is very difficult to delegate responsibility for entrepreneurial activities; and if you do, you may lose effective control of your business.

> The more you delegate your routine activities to others, the more time you will be able to devote to the entrepreneurial planning aspects of the business

PLANNING AND CONTROL

Effective entrepreneurial planning assumes that no important decision will be made without your knowledge and approval. Constantly changing conditions will require that you have adequate control of your business. An important purpose of business planning is to enable you to have the right information at the right time in order to make the right decisions.[1]

Personal involvement in all aspects of business is usually not possible, and would not be an efficient use of your time. It is important for you to have tight control over the more entrepreneurial aspects of the business and to delegate control of all other aspects of it to your staff. Once your staff have demonstrated that they are capable of assuming responsibilities, delegate authority to them.

Your planning should be based on the primary needs of the business and not on any personal motives. Planning and control of your business will be successful to the extent that these activities are directly related to the needs and objectives of the business.

Good planning results in defining specific goals and objectives, and helps your employees to know what is expected of them. The time you spend in developing, implementing and evaluating the results of planning will help to determine your success.

Business planning can be viewed in two ways: long-term planning and short-term planning. Out of necessity, long-term planning is rather general in terms of projected goals and outcomes. You should have a good idea of where you want your business to be in one or two years. However, circumstances change continually and you must be prepared to adjust your plans accordingly. The ability to engage in short-term planning and to determine and achieve short-term goals are characteristics of most entrepreneurs.

The longer the planning cycle, the more probable it is that new developments will occur to make you change your plans.

Implementing long-term plans may become a real problem unless proper controls are used. As an entrepreneur, you will be responsible for making planning decisions continuously. Try to develop a method or procedure for doing so. You may divide a long-term plan into various phases so that the time-span for any one phase will be short, thus giving you better control over the outcomes of various phases of the long-term plan.

Monitoring the implementation of a long-term plan requires that you establish check-points to ensure that each phase of the plan is completed according to a time schedule. Specific individuals within the organisation should be held accountable for specific aspects of implementing the plan.

---

[1] See Robert Abramson and Walter Halset: *Planning for improved enterprise performance: Guide for managers and consultants* (Geneva, ILO, 1979).

Figure 5. Specimen time schedule: plan for starting a business

Task	Month 1-2-3-4-5-6-7-8-9-10-11-12-13-14-15-16-17-18-19-20-21-22-23-24
1. Decide to go into business	←→
2. Analyse your strengths and weaknesses	←→
3. Select a product or service	←→
4. Conduct market research	←→
5. Assess your potential share of the market	←→
6. Select a location for your business	←→
7. Prepare a financial plan	←→
8. Prepare a production plan	←→
9. Prepare a management plan	←→
10. Prepare a marketing plan	←→
11. Borrow funds to begin	←→

Those accountable for certain outcomes should be given the authority and responsibility needed to complete their tasks successfully.

You may want to make a time schedule for implementing your plans. This time schedule should be simple and easy to use (see figure 5). By identifying on a chart all the tasks necessary to accomplish a plan, and the order in which the tasks must be accomplished, you will have a total picture of what you are doing. This type of chart will be helpful in your planning activities, because it will help to identify what tasks are important and when each task has to be accomplished. Establishing time-limits for completing each task will give you additional motivation to accomplish the task within the given time schedule.

> Good planning includes controls necessary to implement the plan successfully. Although long-term plans may be changed, they provide direction for all business activities

ACCOUNTABILITY

One result of good planning is that you will have specific factors to evaluate performance in the completion of tasks. Accountability for your actions and the actions of others is essential to business success. You must know where your organisation is at any given moment, and where it is going. The more control you have over the tasks, the easier the accountability process will be to implement. Keep all persons in your organisation aware of their responsibilities, and review each person's accomplishments regularly. If everyone knows he will be held accountable for his work, and is expected to perform at a specific level, he will be more likely to produce good results.

In most instances, your evaluation of performance should be in measurable terms, such as the number of products made in one day or total sales per week. The way you describe the evaluation data will help to analyse and determine what the data indicate.

Planning brings purpose and a sense of order to your actions as an entrepreneur. The process of accountability implies that most persons do their best when their work is evaluated on a regular, formal and objective basis. Accountability also implies that your employees will perform at an acceptable level.

Planning helps to establish precise outcomes as a result of completing specific tasks. Success in business is more certain if proper planning is undertaken and if each individual in the organisation is aware of his responsibility for specific tasks

---

PLANNING FOR BUSINESS GROWTH

In most businesses, planning for growth is the responsibility of top management. These plans are usually general and provide guidelines for the operation of the business. Planning, however, should be the responsibility of all members of an organisation. The more people there are in an organisation, the more possibilities there are for people to be involved in the planning process.

Top and middle management should have more freedom to determine goals than lower levels of management in the organisational structure. The goals and tasks become more specific at the lower organisational levels, such as supervisor, foreman and shop-floor worker. Although planning will benefit everyone in an organisation, the amount of time a person spends in planning will be determined by his or her job. The higher people progress in an organisation, the more time they spend on the planning aspects of the business, and the less time they spend on the operating aspects of the business. The following diagram illustrates this idea:

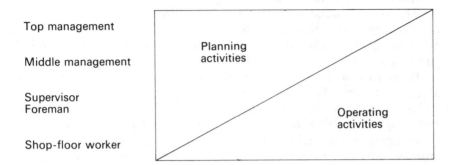

Planning for action is quite different from the action itself. Given a choice, most people would spend more time in "doing" rather than in "planning". The question is: "Are you engaged in activities which will be most beneficial to the over-all needs of your business?"

Planning, an essential but difficult task for anyone in business, is similar to problem-solving. First, you must establish goals. Next, you need to gather information and data relating to the proposed goals. Then, you must determine the best strategy possible to achieve these goals and develop specific tasks to accomplish each goal. Achievement of each task must be evaluated, and alternative courses of action may have to be implemented if the results are not satisfactory.

It is easy to implement action, once appropriate planning has taken place. Without planning, however, your decisions will be made according to current conditions rather than being based on long-term goals.

Listing the objectives, arranging them in order of importance, and identifying sub-objectives will be helpful in preparing an over-all business plan. Each objective should have a list of tasks necessary for its accomplishment. In some instances the task necessary to achieve one objective may be needed to achieve other objectives as well.

Plans may be established three to four months in advance of their implementation. This procedure will force you to think about the future and have adequate plans for your organisation. When planning ahead, you will probably have to make changes in the plans. However, planning helps you to prepare your organisation for the future with some degree of certainty. Planning gives purpose to your actions. Past plans and actions can provide useful information for future planning.

General economic conditions may help to determine business success. If economic conditions are good, even poorly organised businesses may be successful. If economic conditions are poor, only a small proportion of businesses may be able to maintain their success. Planning will help to ensure that your organisation will be successful and that it will grow irrespective of outside economic conditions.

Try to understand the broad trends within your particular industry. Because new techniques and innovations are always being introduced, planning must include provisions for new product development to help you to stay ahead of your competitors.

Plans should include a commitment to experiment with new techniques and methods. A commitment to try something new should be undertaken on a limited basis, involving the least amount of time, money and energy as possible; and it should be monitored and evaluated closely.

Planning should include provisions for the organisation to expand its business into new markets. Personnel should be alert to new ways of marketing and advertising to reach new groups of potential customers.

A certain amount of conformity by employees is necessary in a well organised company. However, people should be encouraged to use their creative talents to improve the company's business methods and procedures.

To some extent, everyone should be involved in planning. Those who make significant contributions to the planning process should receive some form of recognition. Everyone in an organisation should be involved in self-development, and this book is intended to help individuals do just that. As individual performances improve, the organisation will benefit.

The most important asset of an organisation is its people. If they are action-oriented and capable of making independent decisions, the business will have the ingredients necessary for growth. To keep energetic and talented personnel, the organisation should encourage people to be involved in the planning process as well as to assume responsibility for taking action to accomplish these plans.

> Planning for business growth is never dull or routine. Growth implies change and requires a creative and talented entrepreneur to develop a better organisation

ESTABLISHING PRIORITIES

Business planning involves the establishment of priorities. If your business is having problems, there are certain key areas where planning efforts will have immediate effects on the business. For example, in most businesses costs can be reduced and large savings can be made. It is vital that money should be spent in the most efficient way.

If savings are to be made, they should be selective rather than across the board. Proper planning will ensure that the costs which contribute the least will be reduced first.

Review costs of the following types to see where reductions might be made:

- [ ] *direct costs*, such as labour and material to produce the product or service;
- [ ] *indirect costs*, such as supplies and labour which are not directly used in producing a product or service, and overhead factory expenses for light and heat;
- [ ] *administrative costs*, such as office expenses and management and staff salaries; and
- [ ] *sales expenses*, which include all costs involved in selling the product or service such as advertising, the salaries and expenses of sales staff, and sales promotion.

If a business is successful and expands too quickly, there is a danger that those key aspects of the business which made it successful may be neglected and that the sales and profits may decline. Planning for expansion becomes a major factor in determining the future success of a business.

New product development should be another item to be included in business planning. As a business owner, you must make the assumption that your competitors and other people who are interested in starting businesses are constantly seeking products or services to produce. These innovations will make your products or services obsolete unless you are making improvements in your business.

Each of the above cost areas can be divided into separate parts. Be able to identify areas where costs are high and low. Keeping this information on a weekly basis will help you to monitor these costs and see where changes have occurred. Knowing where the costs are greatest, or where costs have recently increased, is one way of identifying places where costs might be reduced.

People who start businesses are usually involved in all aspects of operating them. As growth takes place, you should become less involved in the day-to-day activities, and begin delegating authority and responsibility to others. This process, taking place over a period of time, may lead to changes in operating procedures. If they do, you must ensure that everyone affected knows of the changes and is aware of his or her new role and responsibilities.

Delegating routine activities to your staff will allow you to spend your time on more important aspects of the business. No matter how large or small your business is, it is essential that you plan the use of your time. Planning will help you to identify those activities which will require most of your attention and time

---

USING TIME EFFECTIVELY

6

> Time is something that you cannot save: you simply lose more and more of it as the day progresses. By the end of the day there is none left to use! All entrepreneurs need to manage time effectively, and the key to using time effectively is through better management

By budgeting time you will achieve better results. Specific ways to make better use of your time include establishing goals; determining deadlines; allocating time for each important activity.

Creativity, problem-solving and opportunity-seeking are the hall-marks of entrepreneurs. You must therefore set aside time for activities of these kinds; and all other duties should be given lower priority and be carried out later. You must use time effectively to accomplish those things which you believe are most important.

> You have no choice whether or not to save or spend time! Time is one of your greatest assets, but *time must be spent*. The main concern of this chapter is to identify techniques for spending your time effectively

GOAL-SETTING

To understand the idea of mastering your own time, divide time into two categories: time determined by outside influences; and time determined through your personal control.

Setting daily goals (in terms of outside influences and personal control) is the keystone to scheduling your time. If your daily goals are specific and attainable, you will have a sense of purpose during the day and a sense of accomplishment at the end of each day. Because each of us is unique, goal-setting and time-scheduling will differ for each individual. Develop daily goals and activity schedules to satisfy your own needs.

All goals should be time-phased. Once you are aware of time as a factor in setting goals, you will recognise that time-limits have to be established by making decisions about the importance of each goal. Bear in mind that setting goals, determining priorities and establishing time-limits for achieving each goal are creative and productive activities.

You must be goal-oriented in the sense that you have long-term as well as short-term goals. Instead of beginning the day by tackling less important jobs, concentrate first on the major issues, whether they are easy or not. Once these have been dealt with—whether intermediate, short- or long-term—the rest of your activities can be undertaken.

The more general your goal, the harder it is to be precise about the amount of time needed to achieve it. From time to time you may have to revise your time-plan; and in so doing you will come closer to successful achievement. By ignoring the time element you run the risk of failure.

> The key to efficient use of time lies in identifying *important* goals. When your goal has been clearly identified, the activities which will lead to it should be defined in sequence. Make the first activity as easy as possible; completing it will give you confidence to proceed

THE TIME PROBLEM

One way to increase productive use of time is to initiate several activities which occur simultaneously. For example, four related activities can be undertaken by your staff while you deal only with problems of major importance.

You must not only use *your* time effectively; you must also be interested in the effective use of your organisation's time. Time is one of your organisation's greatest assets. However, it is up to you to make *time* an essential asset for all your employees.

Entrepreneurs should spend most of their time on those objectives and problems which affect the organisation as a whole. However, be on your guard against spending too much time on the problems with which you are most familiar and avoiding problems with which you are least familiar. You must identify the *major* problems facing your organisation and tackle them in priority order, giving preference to short-term rather than long-term problems.

> Profits keep your business alive. Any problems affecting profits *must* be dealt with before other problems are tackled

TIME MANAGEMENT TECHNIQUES

Time management is similar to good work habits. To make the best use of time simply means achieving the maximum output in the time available. There are several ways in which this can be done.

☐ *Identify daily specific goals.* Make sure you understand what you want to accomplish each day. Before arriving, or as soon as you get to work, list your work goals in order of importance. Start working on your most important goal first, setting aside all other work until this is achieved. Don't let outside influences stop you from accomplishing your goal.

Major goals may require total concentration; try, therefore, to work on your own until the goal is achieved. Avoid interruptions and distractions. Your office routines should be established so as to operate without your being there. If office matters constantly interrupt your concentration, changes are needed.

☐ *Self-motivation.* Entrepreneurs are usually highly motivated individuals who seem to enjoy work regardless of what they do. Most people are able to accomplish goals which are similar to what they *want* to do. However, entrepreneurs are able to motivate themselves to produce high outputs in work which they *have* to do.

☐ *Establish deadlines.* More work can be done if you set specific deadlines to achieve certain tasks. But make sure that the deadlines are realistic. Once they are set, you should do everything possible to meet the deadlines.

☐ *Use the telephone.* The telephone is the main communication link between you and your working world. Letters are sometimes necessary, but keep them to a minimum. Problems can be solved more quickly by using the telephone. A letter provides only one-way communication while a telephone conversation is two-way communication. In some circumstances it may be worth while to record the conversation on a tape-recorder.

☐ *Take notes.* Keep a note-pad handy at all times. Writing down key points provides a permanent record of committee meetings, telephone conversations, discussions with staff or business clients, or simply your own thoughts. Record thoughts and ideas and jot down such things as future appointments, things to do, names and telephone numbers.

☐ *Don't do everything.* An old saying is: "If you want something done, have a busy person do it." Entrepreneurs are busy, but their actions are purposeful. Concentrate only on important activities. By being goal-oriented, you should do those activities which lead to significant results. Be selective in your work activities and try not to do everything. Learn to say "no" to time-consuming activities not directly connected with your priority goals.

☐ *Work in blocks of time.* Try to do major tasks in blocks of time (three or four hours) during the period of the day when you feel most effective. Schedule your other activities around these blocks of time. If the block of time goes through lunch, eat a good breakfast and miss lunch. Working undisturbed for three or four hours can be very productive when dealing with a special problem or situation. Although it may be difficult to allocate a block of time for one activity, it will often be the only way in which to solve a particular problem.

☐ *Ask questions before beginning work.* Almost any work can be done more efficiently. Before beginning, make sure you have answers to such questions as: What? Where? When? Who? How? Why? The answers to these questions will help you to find more efficient ways of accomplishing your work. For each step in an activity, ask yourself: "Why do I need to do this?" Your answers will help to determine the most essential tasks of the activity.

☐ *Be action-oriented.* Once you have decided to solve a specific problem, outline your specific course of action and then get on with it. Once you begin, try to complete as much as you can as soon as possible. In other words, take time to plan your work and then take time to work your plan.

  This action orientation should help you to stop procrastinating about tackling a problem. Moreover, if you view each problem as an opportunity for potential improvement, you will be more aware of innovative and creative ways of solving the problem.

☐ *Be reflective.* Reflective thinking is the act of learning from one's past, present and potential future activities. Most of us do not think very much about what we do, and finding time to be reflective is very difficult. However, there are times when it is possible for you to be alone with your own thoughts and ideas, such as when resting before sleeping; travelling; waiting for transport; or walking alone. Use these times to reflect on your work.

☐ *Plan in detail for tomorrow.* At the end of each day's work, prepare a time schedule for the following day's activities. You might even be able to begin one activity, thus providing you with a flying start to the next day and reducing the danger of procrastination. It is sometimes easier to complete than to begin an activity! The end of the day is also a good time to examine ways in which you wasted time or used it inefficiently. Write down these time-wasters and you will be less likely to make the same mistakes in the future.

☐ *Learn from your experiences.* Reviewing your past experiences helps to determine which of them were interesting and productive and which were dull, time-consuming and unproductive. You will face similar experiences in the future, and it is up to you to choose only those activities which will be most worth while and productive.

☐ *Question your use of time.* In order to manage time properly, ask the following questions:

— What activities am I doing that I should not be doing or should be delegated to others?

— Do I set priorities when I am deciding which activities to do?

— Are my activities scheduled so that they can be accomplished in a reasonable amount of time?

— Am I able to concentrate on one activity at a time?

Try to remember good techniques of time management. These time-saving techniques will help to improve your entrepreneurial performance.

Remember these time-savers:

Identify specific goals	Work in blocks of time
Be motivated	Ask questions
Establish deadlines	Be action-oriented
Use the telephone	Do reflective thinking
Take notes	Be ready for each day's work
Do only essential activities	Learn from past experiences

Question your use of time

TIME-SAVING TIPS

The following tips may help you to save time:

☐ Schedule committee meetings and business conferences as close to lunch or dinner as possible. Most people will be keen to complete the meeting on time!

☐ Keep a simple filing system. Review your files periodically and discard those you no longer need.

☐ Instruct your secretary to screen telephone calls so that you answer only those which are absolutely essential. Alternatively, ask your secretary to take messages to be answered by you later in the day.

☐ Keep your desk clear. Except for the materials you are actually using, keep everything else out of sight. Other materials and notes can distract, and removing them should reduce the tendency to try to do more than one thing at a time. By seeing only materials dealing with one activity, your concentration will be focused more sharply on the job in hand.

☐ Identify your key hours of the day. The first working hour of the day can be most productive if devoted to your highest priority activity. The lunchtime hour is generally quiet in an office, and this period can be used productively. The hour before finishing work can be used for routine things such as dictating letters, making telephone calls, reading reports, and preparing for the next day's activities.

☐ You purposely may take on more activities than you think you can accomplish. This forces you to think of ways to economise on your time.

An essential characteristic of an entrepreneur is the ability to operate in an organised manner. *To other people, it may appear that the entrepreneur is highly disorganised.* However, the subconscious mind of most entrepreneurs is highly active. When you understand that the productive use of time is essential to your being entrepreneurial, you will realise that time is one of your greatest assets

---

REDUCING TIME PRESSURES

To deal with daily pressures in personal as well as working life, you need to use effective techniques of time management. The technology of business has made rapid advances and will continue to do so in the future. Not all human beings can keep up with these technological advances. The entrepreneur is a good example of someone able to cope with change, adapt to an ever-changing environment, be productive and obtain good results by using time management.

Being completely preoccupied with day-to-day business problems can produce great pressures and stress; but applying principles of time management can relieve some of these pressures.

Like most managers, you will probably have a long list of things to do daily, weekly and monthly. These include attending meetings, supervising others, giving orders, writing reports and memos, and a multitude of other duties. You need a systematic means of dealing with these activities, otherwise much pressure and frustration may develop.

Figure 6. Mastering time

Goals	Time period
Short-term	One hour Two hours One day One week
Intermediate	Two weeks Three weeks One month
Long-term	More than one month

One solution for reducing the pressures created by lack of time is organising and using time through planning. *Short-term* planning may be done on a regular basis and should outline specific objectives for each day of the week, whereas planning on a *long-term* basis will pertain to goals over one month (see figure 6).

A written plan designating short-term, intermediate and long-term goals will provide the basis for an organised approach to time management and help to reduce the tension, stress and pressures of your job. Making progress towards your stated goals is a way of reducing anxiety and tension. By monitoring progress on a regular basis during the day (perhaps every 30 minutes), you can get immediate feedback and positive reinforcement. It is important to reflect from time to time on your own activities and the conditions in which you undertake them. This "self-management" should help you to detect anything preventing successful achievement.

For example, your working conditions might be distracting, thus creating tension or frustration. The effects will vary, according to one's feelings, location and condition. Negative physical factors in the environment may include noise, cigarette smoke, temperature, lighting conditions, and other people. People often create the biggest problems by complaining, criticising, arguing, laughing, or by constantly talking and being disruptive.

If you believe you are working in a negative environment, you will have to take the initiative to change it. Listing options of change will provide alternatives for creating a more positive work environment, and a change in one of your activities could lead to changes in other activities.

ORGANISATIONAL IMPROVEMENTS

Time spent thinking about the future of your organisation may be very productive. The following key questions may offer opportunities for improving your organisation.

The future of the organisation

- [ ] What economic trends during the next five years might affect my business?
- [ ] What new products and/or services do I plan to develop during the next five years?
- [ ] What research is being conducted which might affect my business operations?
- [ ] To what extent will new technology have an impact on labour requirements for the next five years?
- [ ] In what ways might the organisation change during the next five years?

Future personnel needs

- [ ] In what new ways might the performance of the personnel be evaluated?
- [ ] How can I improve the performance of key personnel working in the organisation?
- [ ] What plans are there to develop for key employees the management skills which they will need in the future?
- [ ] What staff personnel are responsible for preparing the organisational changes needed in the future?
- [ ] What elements of the personnel development programme help to prepare the organisation for the future?

Organisational needs

- [ ] What are some ways to improve the present organisation?
- [ ] Why do some departments of the organisation operate more efficiently than others?
- [ ] How are efficiency and effectiveness measured in the various departments such as sales, research and production?
- [ ] How can I measure the total organisation's performance?
- [ ] How can working relationships between departments be improved?
- [ ] How can the morale of the organisation be improved?
- [ ] How can the organisation's internal communications be improved?

> Whenever you have free time, you will probably be thinking about some aspect of your business. During this time, ask yourself questions to help to focus on specific business problems and to identify solutions to each problem

THE "TO DO" LIST

A "To Do" list serves as a good reminder. Some people use a small writing pad or diary. Others use a small sheet of paper. Another way to organise your "To Do" list is to design your form to meet specific needs. Figure 7 is one example of a "To Do" form. This form could be duplicated on a small card and be kept in your pocket, purse or wallet. The reverse side of the card could be used for comments and other notes. A "To Do" list provides a simple, effective way of organising your tasks so that they can be accomplished in order of priority. As each task is completed, draw a single line through the task, or tick it. The "To Do" list identifies what is to be done and in what order the tasks should be completed.

Figure 7. "To Do" form

THINGS "TO DO"   Date:_____

Main task for today: _____

Priority	Things "To Do"

Appointments

Name	Address	Telephone no.

ANALYSING YOUR USE OF TIME

Developing a chart to write down specific activities is one way of determining whether your activities are essential or non-essential. An example of such a Time Chart is shown in figure 8. There is space for 16

Figure 8. Time Chart

TIME CHART			
Main task: _____		Date: _____	
_____		Day: _____	
Time	Goal	Activity	Outcome
: 00			
: 30			
: 00			
: 30			
: 00			
: 30			
: 00			
: 30			
: 00			
: 30			
: 00			
: 30			
: 00			
: 30			
: 00			
: 30			
: 00			
: 30			
: 00			
: 30			
: 00			
: 30			
: 00			
: 30			
: 00			
: 30			
: 00			
: 30			
: 00			
: 30			
: 00			
: 30			

hours of activities (the average number of hours most people are awake). The Time Chart is divided into 30-minute segments; it is your responsibility to write in the hour in the "time" column, since people begin their daily activities at different times.

The Time Chart has space to record time, activity, goal and outcome. Each activity performed should have a definite goal, with the result recorded in the "outcome" column. The length of "time" and "outcome" in relation to "goal" will give some evidence of effectiveness of using time for any given activity. At the end of each day, tick those activities which were not essential and try to avoid them in the future.

Using the Time Chart for one month will show exactly how you used your time in relation to your goals. In some instances, you may be doing things which are in no way related to your main goals. Only by being aware of the importance of time can you make your activities purposeful. The box at the top of the Time Chart has enough space to indicate the main task for the day and the date. Concentrating on achieving the main task will help you to accomplish positive results by the end of each day.

If it is possible for you to use a daily Time Chart for three or four weeks, you should be able to determine how much time you spend on various activities, the types of objectives you believe are important, and the outcome of your various activities. Weekends can be included as part of the standard week.

There are many things that can be accomplished during the week. The results given on the Time Chart for a period of one month can assist in reviewing past activities and provide guidelines for your future activities so that time is used more efficiently.

The ways in which time can be wasted include:

☐ chatting with people about personal matters unconnected with work;
☐ unnecessary or protracted group meetings;
☐ allowing too many interruptions;
☐ disorganisation;
☐ little or no delegating;
☐ being indecisive; and
☐ being late or absent.

Successful entrepreneurs use time effectively. Once spent, time can never be recovered. To be more entrepreneurial, use every minute of every waking hour productively. Planning, organising and scheduling are the keys to successful time management. Remember, one of the few things you can really control is the use of your time

If the above time-wasters can be decreased by using daily Time Charts, your personal efficiency will be increased. Once you know how you spent your time in the past, it will be easier to plan the use of your time in the future. A definite plan for using time will help you to become more effective in achieving your personal work-goals.

FINANCIAL PLANNING AND CONTROL

An entrepreneur may have difficulty with the financial side of his business. Part II is designed to identify the proper attitudes and behaviour you should adopt toward your financial affairs. The need for measuring and controlling your results in financial terms is essential.

Part II includes:

7. Financial action plans
8. Developing value attitudes towards resources
9. Measuring and controlling financial strategies and results
10. Financial success through people
11. Tools for control and decisions: information systems

One of the key areas for entrepreneurial success is financial planning and control. The planning and control of the financial affairs of a business are critical to its future. Entrepreneurs must spend time in improving the financial position of their business: eliminating weaknesses, developing strengths, learning from past successes and mistakes, and organising its future financial development.

Another essential aspect of business activity is the control of the results of your business activities. You must be willing to take action, invest financial resources, measure outcomes and take corrective action when needed. At all times, you must be able to find and use financial resources which will contribute to your business growth and development.

Information is the key to making most financial decisions in your business; to have proper information flow, you must develop information systems which keep your employees informed, help them to become involved, and motivate them to improve performance standards.

The purpose of this Part is to illustrate possible methods of financial planning and control rather than to prescribe a particular method. The methods illustrated are based on the more common approaches followed in English-speaking countries.

FINANCIAL ACTION PLANS

7

> Entrepreneurial action means planning and control. Entrepreneurs identify those aspects of the business which are vital to its future development. They are always eager to improve performance—to eliminate weaknesses; increase strengths; learn from both successes and failures; and plan and organise the company's future

It is important for the entrepreneur to be positive in planning for the future; and in this chapter the emphasis is on *action* as a direct result of financial planning, which includes the following ten steps:

- ☐ setting appropriate financial goals for your business;
- ☐ evaluating alternative financial strategies;
- ☐ collecting and evaluating financial facts and figures to complete the plans;
- ☐ setting efficiency levels and targets (both short- and long-term) for the enterprise, expressed in terms of rewards for owners and employees;
- ☐ developing an over-all financial plan to provide the "big picture" for the future;
- ☐ verifying the over-all plan by examining each component to ensure that each is realistic in the light of past experience;
- ☐ analysing the plan by comparing it with established standards of performance, both internal and external;
- ☐ reviewing the plan, revising it as necessary until an acceptable combination of strategies and factors has been achieved;
- ☐ using the plan as a motivating force by communicating the results of planning to key personnel at all stages in the process; and
- ☐ ensuring that the planning process is followed up by adequate control, and informing and motivating the staff involved.

These ten steps can be condensed and are incorporated in the following seven stages:

☐ produce short- and long-term financial targets;

☐ set short- and long-term financial rewards;

☐ set efficiency standards covering all facets of the operations;

☐ document the over-all financial plan;

☐ verify the plan, revising it where necessary;

☐ analyse the plan and make comparisons between it and established standards; and

☐ communicate the plan to employees and prepare for the reporting and control stage.

STAGE 1: GOAL-SETTING: FINANCIAL FIGURES FOR LONG-TERM TARGETS

Although business goals may be expressed in financial and non-financial terms, we shall focus on *financial* goals. Being entrepreneurial, you will want to "put pen to paper" to quantify your ideas on business growth, strategies, percentage returns, rewards, product/services diversification, and the like. You are quantifying and measuring the impact of growth, strategies, product changes, new outlets, changes in promotion, the impact of advertising, and so on. The entrepreneur questions "What is?" and is continuously asking "What if?"; and he expects direct answers.

However, there is more to entrepreneurial goal-setting than putting pen to paper. The process itself helps you to come to grips with your environment. As you set goals for profitability, you assess *your* business in its industrial environment. As you set goals for efficiency, you are assessing the *quality* of your total resources: personnel, equipment, plant. As you set goals for growth, you are pitching your business against others in the market-place. In other words, setting goals is a business review process.

Now let us get down to some details, with examples. Your financial goals could include statements on some or all of the following:

~~~~~~

A statement of financial goals: XYZ Corporation

Financial goals: business profitability

The enterprise will remain profitable in the face of fluctuating economic and market conditions. Net profits earned each year are expected to increase at a rate in excess of the annual cost-of-living indices after adjustments for fluctuating risk assessments. Profits must be sufficient to reward owners and employees, provide an acceptable return on investment, and allow annual reinvestment of funds in line with growth expectations.

Financial goals: business efficiency

Various efficiency measures will be used to assess financial performance; and targets will be set and revised from year to year taking into consideration market conditions, personal experience and expertise. Over-all efficiency measures will relate net profit before taxation to sales revenue and business investment. The business expects to achieve results for these two efficiency measures that are equivalent to results reported for the top 10 per cent of the industry. The business expects to maintain or improve its relative position in the industry. Under current conditions, it appears that appropriate short-term performance standards for these two ratios will be:

Net margin: 10 per cent   Return on investment: 30 per cent

Long-term projections suggest that net margin ratios should steadily increase to 15 per cent and return on investment decrease with declining risk (to, say, 25 per cent) over the following ten years.

Efficiency measures for capital and people productivity will be established for each division within our enterprise.

Financial goals: growth expectations

Sales revenue, product penetration, profits and owner's equity will be expected to increase annually. Sales revenue will be expected to increase at a rate exceeding the economy's wholesale price indices and at a rate equivalent to that achieved by all firms in the upper 10 per cent of the industry. Product market shares will increase until (at least) 60 per cent of the market has been obtained. Net profits will increase by a rate exceeding the consumer price indices and a rate at least equal to the upper 10 per cent of the industry. Owner's equity will increase by a rate exceeding the growth in stock exchange indices.

Financial goals: rewards to owners

Financial rewards to owners will consist of a *time reward* reflecting hours allocated to the business, owner experience, qualifications and responsibility; and a *reward for investment* reflecting changing risks associated with the business. Time rewards will be related to the opportunity cost of managerial competence, and investment rewards will be related to alternative investment opportunities in the market-place. Time rewards are expected to be at least $20,000 per annum and risk return on investment in the short term at least 30 per cent, reducing to 25 per cent over a period of time, with falling business risk.

Financial goals: rewards to employees

The enterprise aims to hire and retain the most efficient and effective personnel, whose personal goals are in line with those of the corporation. With this in mind, every effort will be made to develop each individual within the organisation, and to reward each in line with hours worked, productivity, experience, qualifications and responsibility accepted. Employees can expect to share in the rewards of increased productivity.

Financial goals: investment

In current replacement terms, at least 60 per cent of all assets acquired will be financed through owner's equity—new investment capital or reinvested profits. In the short term, return on owner's equity will be at least 30 per cent and in the long term (with reduced risk) at least 25 per cent. This implies that all new *assets* purchased will produce return expectations of at least 18 per cent in the short term, and 15 per cent in the long term. All revenue-producing assets requiring an expenditure exceeding $20,000 must project these targets. Cost-saving assets will be expected to produce returns higher than these standards.

Financial goals: . . . .

And so our list of goals and targets could continue. The document should be prepared in more detail. Some items could be excluded. Standards may vary from year to year. Over-all philosophy is important. Goals are essential as starting-points in the planning and control process. Without goals, the entrepreneur has no base, no bench-marks to use in the improvement process; no opportunity to detect weaknesses; no opportunity to build on strengths; little opportunity to learn from experience; few chances to be "positive".

The goal-setting process is an exercise in discipline, not unlike the planning process itself. Goal-setting is *your* job as the entrepreneur. Many members of your staff will be involved in the planning process, but you must accept responsibility for goal-setting. Both you and your staff must allocate time to short-term and long-term planning and goal-setting. In an arbitrary fashion, we could take the goal-setting process and other tasks in the planning process and make the following allocations indicating relative emphases:

	Planning time spent in short-term planning	Planning time spent in long-term planning
	%	%
The entrepreneur (YOU)	20	80
Senior support staff	50	50
Lower-level management	90	10

So the goals are set! Now the planning details need to be specific. The next stage is to set financial rewards for the short and the long term.

STAGE 2: A STATEMENT OF FINANCIAL REWARDS: XYZ CORPORATION

Next year

The financial reward for the owner will consist of a *time* reward and an *investment return* reward. The *time* reward will be calculated as:

	$
Basic managerial salary	15 000
Loading for hours worked	2 000
Qualifications	500
Experience	1 500
Responsibility	3 000
Total	22 000

The financial return on *investment* reward will be based on a return of 30 per cent for an investment of $127,000 = $38,100.

Total financial reward for the following year will therefore be $60,100.

Long term

Basic managerial salary will be indexed quarterly in line with national wage increases, and loadings will be adjusted in line with length of experience, qualifications, responsibilities, and an annual industry survey of executive salaries as carried out by professional associations. Given current trends, the following represents *expected* owner reward projections for the five years that follow:

	Year 1	Year 2	Year 3	Year 4	Year 5
	$	$	$	$	$
Time	24 000	28 400	33 000	35 000	40 000
Investment	39 000	42 000	45 000	50 800	53 800
Total	63 000	70 400	78 000	85 800	93 800

For *your* business, details of investment and returns could be expanded. What is important is your attitude to the reward-setting process. It is not a question of increasing the cash available to you *per se*; rather, the plan expresses the confidence you have in your own ability, with the support of your staff, to achieve "acceptable" and "justifiable" reward figures. In setting rewards, you are being entrepreneurial.

Stage 3 in the exercise is to set standards of business efficiency, and these will be used to determine your over-all financial plan.

STAGE 3: EFFICIENCY STANDARDS

Various efficiency standards will be discussed later in this chapter. For purposes of this example, targets are limited to gross margins, expenses and net margins. Targets may be established from internal records and from industry statistics. The latter are often referred to as "external" or "inter-business" comparisons. Both sets of data are important for the entrepreneur since constant comparisons between your business and others in the industry are in line with the concept of building on strengths, eliminating weaknesses and taking positive attitudes to growth. You *need* industry statistics. With this in mind, the following tables, representing past and projected data, may be useful in your planning process:

Relative performance: XYZ Corporation

	Year −3	Year −2	Year −1	Base year	Year +1	Year +2	Year +3	Year +4	Year +5
	%	%	%	%	%	%	%	%	%
Sales	100	100	100	100	100	100	100	100	100
Cost of sales	75	75	74	73	73	73	72	72	71
Gross margin	25	25	26	27	27	27	28	28	29
Expenses	18	17	17	17	17	16	16	15	15
Net margin	7	8	9	10	10	11	12	13	14

Relative performance: other corporations (inter-business)

	Year −3	Year −2	Year −1	Base year	Year +1	Year +2	Year +3	Year +4	Year +5
	%	%	%	%	%	%	%	%	%
Sales	100	100	100	100	100	100	100	100	100
Cost of sales	74	74	73	73	72	72	72	72	71
Gross margin	26	26	27	27	28	28	28	28	29
Expenses	17	17	17	17	16	16	16	15	15
Net margin	9	9	10	10	12	12	12	13	14

Given the internal and external statistics of past performance and future expectations, the entrepreneur can now develop an *over-all* financial plan. The relative figures are applied to the financial rewards requirements to establish sales, expenses and profit projections.

STAGE 4: PUTTING TOGETHER THE OVER-ALL FINANCIAL PLAN

Given net margin percentage targets and required owner's rewards, it is possible to project sales targets for each of the following six years together with related expense and net profit figures. In detail, for the base year:

Required net margin target = 10 per cent

Required entrepreneurial reward = $60 100

Therefore, sales target = $601 000 ($60 100 × 10 per cent)

Given these figures, the over-all financial plan for the year can be put together:

	$	%
Sales	601 000	100
Cost of sales	438 730	73
Gross margin	162 270	27
Expenses	102 170	17
Net margin	60 100	10

This exercise can be repeated for each year of the forward plan, and your future financial growth picture for your enterprise unfolds:

	Base year	Year +1	Year +2	Year +3	Year +4	Year +5
	$	$	$	$	$	$
Sales	601 000	630 000	640 000	650 000	660 000	670 000
Cost of sales	438 730	459 900	467 200	468 000	475 200	475 700
Gross margin	162 270	170 100	172 800	182 000	184 800	194 300
Expenses	102 170	107 100	102 400	104 000	99 000	100 500
Net margin	60 100	63 000	70 400	78 000	85 800	93 800

These key facts will enable you to exercise control over the future of your enterprise. You should *not* be involved with expenditure details or sales details but rather with *total* sales and total expenditure. You set the guidelines; your staff are to ensure that your enterprise achieves required targets.

STAGE 5: VERIFYING THE PLAN

Being entrepreneurial, you will not be content to document the over-all financial plan without having it checked and cross-checked as "being achievable". If sales targets for the base year are $601,000, what product lines will be an acceptable mix? If a gross margin of 27 per cent is the target, how can this be achieved? What strategy for pricing and stockturn will produce the planned result? Does the strategy call for higher selling prices or more efficient buying of goods for sale, or both?

The entrepreneur will want to see an analysis of product sales, buying prices and margins. During the budget period he will want a counting analysis of actual margins compared with the approved plan. Sales staff will be given specific responsibilities and instructions to ensure targets are met. The following table illustrates the type of analysis which could be used to verify margins:

		Base year	
Product group	Expected sales	Margins	Gross profit
	($)	(%)	($)
A	130 000	30	39 000
B	190 000	25	47 500
C	80 000	33	26 400
D	70 000	26	18 200
E	70 000	31	21 700
F	60 100	15.5	9 470
Total	601 000	27	162 270

Is the sales level for each product group possible? Are margins reasonable? How are they to be achieved? What does the above mean for sales group supervisors?

Verifying the over-all plan requires an analysis of total expenses into components that have some relevance for the control of your business. Classifications of expenses common for taxation purposes may *not* be relevant for decision-making and control purposes by the entrepreneurial manager. The following groups *may* be appropriate:

☐ *Wages and salaries.* Analysed by personel—each staff member to be identified by salary class;

☐ *Occupancy expense.* Analysed by type of expense, i.e. rent, electricity, heating, cleaning, security, insurance;

☐ *Financial expense.* Analysed by type of expense, i.e. interest, discounts, bad debts, bank/lease charges;

☐ *Selling and promotion expenses.* Analysed by type of expense, i.e. advertising, delivery expense, promotion;

☐ *Communication expense.* Analysed by type of expense, i.e. telephone, stationery, telegrams, cables.

In some organisations wages and salaries may be allocated to other expense groups. For example, sales staff salaries may be allocated to selling and promotion expense; clerical and secretarial salaries may be allocated to administration expense; and so on. The approach to be taken should reflect the needs of management.

STAGE 6: ANALYSING THE PLAN

The business plan is analysed to identify weaknesses which may cause financial difficulties in the future; to test alternative strategies for selling, product mix, cost control, investment, staff development, financing, and the like. The analysis is meant to make the entrepreneurial manager answer specific questions about business activities. Methods of analysis can be illustrated by answering a number of questions.

QUESTION: Is the enterprise maintaining an acceptable level of financial efficiency?

ANALYSIS: Ratios for

Net margin: $\dfrac{\text{Net profit}}{\text{Sales}} \times \dfrac{100\%}{1}$

Gross margin: $\dfrac{\text{Gross profit}}{\text{Sales}} \times \dfrac{100\%}{1}$

Expense margin: $\dfrac{\text{Expense}}{\text{Sales}} \times \dfrac{100\%}{1}$

have been illustrated and can be calculated as target figures for your business and comparisons made with industry data.

But being entrepreneurial, you will wish to compare your business's past and future (planned) performance against the top (most efficient) businesses in your industry (see Chapter 9).

QUESTION: Have we reduced the risk of trading loss in our plans?

ANALYSIS: Two ratios can be used to measure trading risk.

1. Break-even point (BEP) for sales—the sales

figures which will cover basic business expenses, i.e. profit is *zero*. The BEP is a sales point to reach *and* pass as soon as possible. It is *one* of many target points for your business. It can be calculated with this formula:

$$\text{BEP} = \frac{\text{Business expenses}}{\text{Gross margin (percentage)}}$$

For example, if your expenses for the year are expected to be $102,000 and the gross margin 27 per cent, your business BEP, in round figures, becomes:

$$\frac{\$102,000}{27\%} = \$377,800$$

Why? Because when your sales reach $377,800, your gross margin will total $27\% \times \$377,800 = \$102,000$, i.e. just enough to cover expenses.

Being entrepreneurial, you will apply the BEP concept to your weekly operations, and to monthly sales. For example, if your basic expenses for each week are (say) $2,000 (salaries, rent, occupancy, etc), your BEP for the week will be sales of $2,000/27\% = \$7,400$. If you then look at your day-to-day sales, you might find that you reach your break-even sales by (say) Friday afternoon, which means that your *profits* for the week will come from sales made on Friday night and Saturday—a sobering thought!

In addition, being entrepreneurial, you will realise also that several BEPs can be calculated for any business: a BEP before *your* salary; BEP by product division; BEP by sales location or sales group.

2. From BEP we move to a ratio referred to as the Margin of Safety (M/S). The M/S is the percentage fall in sales below your expected (planned) sales level before your business reaches its BEP—the zero profit level.

$$\text{M/S} = \frac{\text{Planned sales} - \text{BEP sales}}{\text{Planned sales}} \times \frac{100\%}{1}$$

For example, if your business plan calls for sales of $600,000, and the expense levels and gross margins mean BEP sales of $377,800, your business M/S is:

$$\frac{\$600,000 - \$377,800}{\$600,000} \times \frac{100\%}{1} = 37\%$$

In other words, if sales fall 37 per cent below your plan, you will be at your BEP, i.e. zero profit point.

QUESTION: Is the business financially stable? Have we reduced business financial risk?

ANALYSIS: Several measures are used to indicate financial stability.

1. A common liquidity measure to examine short-term financial stability is the cash ratio:

$$\frac{\text{Cash (or cash equivalent) assets}}{\text{Cash (or cash equivalent) liabilities}}$$
$$= \text{(number of times cover)}$$

For example, if your statement of financial position shows cash, bank balances, debtors (readily convertible to cash), short-term investments and inventory (also readily convertible to cash), totalling $60,000; *and* if liabilities that might have to be met in (say) the next month total $50,000, the liquid ratio becomes:

$$\frac{\$60,000}{\$50,000} = 1.20 \text{ times}$$

Thus, for every $1 owed in short-term liabilities, we have $1.20 in cash or cash equivalent assets—a relatively stable position. A ratio of *less* than 1.00 indicates lack of stability.

2. Are your debtors a risk? Are they a financial burden? To measure the impact of finance tied up in debtor balances, we use a ratio indicating the number of days in credit sales that are outstanding (owing) at a particular point of time. The ratio is calculated in two steps:

   (a) calculate the average credit sales for your business for each trading day:

   e.g. $\dfrac{\$375,000}{250 \text{ days}} = \$1,500$ per day *(b)* calculate the average number of days in credit sales that are outstanding by dividing the $1,500 into the average debtor balances, e.g.

$$\frac{\text{Average debtor balances}}{\text{Average credit sales/day}} = \frac{\$93,000}{\$1,500}$$
$$= 62 \text{ days}$$

Is this acceptable? No! On average, no more than 45 days ($1\frac{1}{2}$ months) of credit sales should be outstanding. In the example given, some corrective action is necessary.

3. Financial leverage! To what extent are assets financed by outside (debt) funds? Leverage is measured by relating:

$$\frac{\text{Current and long-term liabilities (debt)}}{\text{Current and long-term liabilities (debt)} + \text{owner's funds (equity)}}$$

For example, if liabilities total $80,000 and owner's funds $127,000, the leverage ratio becomes:

$$\frac{\$80,000}{\$207,000} \times \frac{100}{1} = 39\%$$

Acceptable? Most entrepreneurs would be looking for a percentage well below 50. The points at issue are: Who controls the assets of the business? Will the interest payable on debt funds be an intolerable burden in the future?

4. Interest cover is measured by relating profit *before* interest expense to the annual interest charge. For example, if your interest charges for the year are expected to be $8,000 and net profit before interest $48,000, interest cover is:

$$\frac{\$48,000}{\$8,000} = 6 \text{ times}$$

Most entrepreneurs would be satisfied with this result—financial risk appears to be very low.

QUESTION: Are inventories under control? Are funds tied up in inventories being used effectively? Could the investment be reduced? Should it be reduced? How do the gross margins and stockturns appear? Are they appropriate?

ANALYSIS: 1. Stockturn is a basic business analysis ratio used by manufacturers, wholesalers and retailers. It is measured as:

$$\frac{Cost \ of \ inventory \ sold \ for \ the \ period}{Average \ inventory \ held \ for \ sale \ during \ the \ period}$$

For example, if the cost of inventory sold for the year was $438,000 and average inventory on hand over the same period $60,000, stockturn is 7.3 times.

$$\frac{\$438,000}{\$60,000} = 7.3 \ times$$

As pointed out earlier, this stockturn ratio should be interpreted in relation to the gross margin. Low margins generally mean high stockturns, and vice versa.

2. As sales increase, inventory should *not* increase at the same rate. Thus a sales growth of 20 per cent may require an inventory growth of only (say) 15 per cent. Thus, a ratio to monitor is your "inventory to sales" percentage.

Other questions could and should be asked and answered; and more ratios are examined in the next chapter. Be entrepreneurial: adapt the use of ratios to *your* business.

STAGE 7: COMMUNICATION THROUGH REPORTS

When you have planned the future strategy for your business, it doesn't make sense to keep all the facts to yourself when you are expecting positive co-operation from your staff. Although questions of (*a*) standard-setting and the control of performance and (*b*) the question of people involvement will be dealt with in Chapters 9 and 10, some basic preliminaries in the visual reporting of financial plans are illustrated in figure 9.

Additional graphs or charts could be prepared for financial stability ratios, productivity, and so on. Many ratios could be converted into visual displays as graphs for communication and control. It is worth remembering that all these visual displays are not only important for the entrepreneur's communication with support staff, but also essential for control because you can plot your *actual* sales, margins, expenses, stockturn, etc., month by month and year by year. The emphasis in each report is on simplicity in presentation of the business overview. Details (of expenses, for example) are left to support staff to control. *You* set standards and set over-all performance; staff control actual sales and expenses within those over-all standards. Too many owners and managers spend too much time working on details that should be left to staff. You must be entrepreneurial!

CASH FLOW

So you have been through the exercise of goal-setting; establishing long-term objectives; converting ideas and plans into financial figures and projections; and finally communicating the results to support staff. Does this spell the end of your entrepreneurial actions? Unfortunately not! One important area of finance needs careful attention: business cash flow, week by week, and month by month. In a nutshell, your carefully prepared profit plans *now:*

☐ are to be converted to weekly/monthly equivalents;

☐ form the starting-point for cash flow projections.

The entrepreneur sees cash as a *resource* to be *managed.* Too many owners and managers leave cash flow to the banks and only know what cash has been received and spent when a bank statement has been received at the end of each month. This is *not* good enough. Controlling cash can increase profits by reducing interest expense; and it means having liquid resources available to take advantage of profitable opportunities. The enterpreneur thrives on opportunities, and therefore must control the availability of cash.

Unfortunately, preparing a cash flow forecast is *not* a simple matter, even if you are equipped with weekly profit projections, because:

☐ Some sales revenue in the weekly profit statement may represent sales on credit, and all credit sales must be converted to cash flow timing (actual cash receipts). A credit sale this week *may* be received in cash in five weeks' time.

☐ Some expenses in weekly profit projections may have been allocated over a number of weeks by your accountant, but may represent a "lump sum" cash payment in a particular week. For example, insurance expense may be allocated over a number of weeks, but may be paid in one amount (say) every six months. Actual payment periods must be identified.

☐ Some expenses appearing in the weekly profit projections may *not* involve any cash flow in the short term. For example, depreciation expense is the cost of using fixed assets (such as plant and equipment) but does not involve weekly cash flow.

Figure 9.   Communication through visual displays: the entrepreneur's over-all view

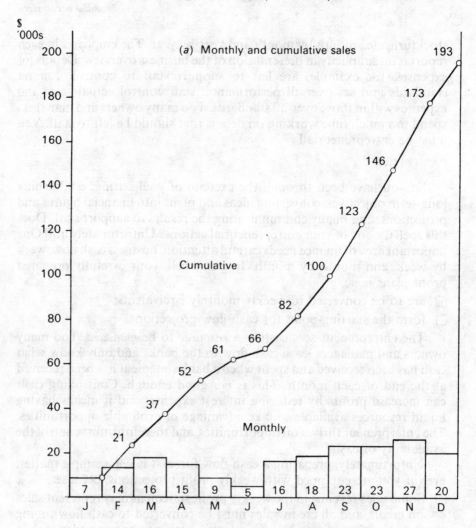

$'000s

(a) Monthly and cumulative sales

Cumulative

Monthly

	J	F	M	A	M	J	J	A	S	O	N	D
	7	14	16	15	9	5	16	18	23	23	27	20

Cumulative values: 21, 37, 52, 61, 66, 82, 100, 123, 146, 173, 193

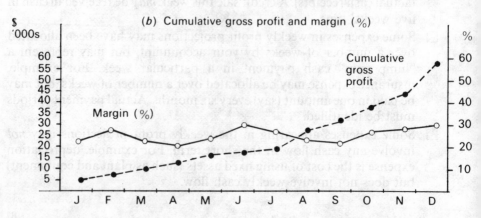

$'000s

(b) Cumulative gross profit and margin (%)

Cumulative gross profit

Margin (%)

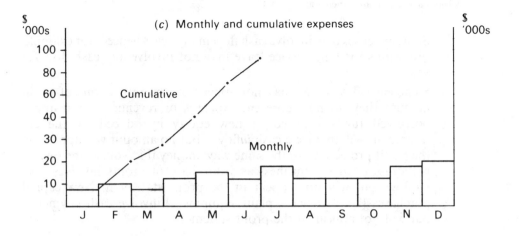

(c) Monthly and cumulative expenses

Cumulative

Monthly

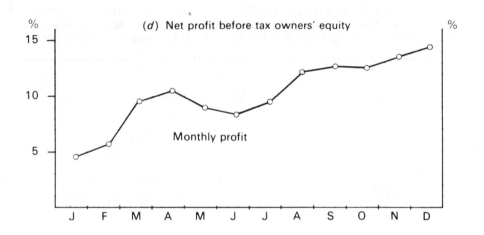

(d) Net profit before tax owners' equity

Monthly profit

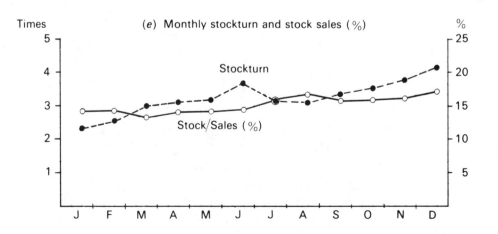

(e) Monthly stockturn and stock sales (%)

Stockturn

Stock/Sales (%)

☐ Some expenses may involve cash flow many years hence—for example, provisions for long-service leave may not involve any cash flow for years to come.

☐ Some cash flow items may not appear on the projections of profit because they do not represent expenses or revenue. For example, borrowed funds received or new equity introduced by the entrepreneur will involve a cash *in*flow—but no amount will appear on the profit projection. In the same way, money that you, as the owner, withdraw from the business as your share of profits involves cash *out*flow, but will not appear in the profit statement. New capital purchases (land, vehicles, plant, equipment) involve cash payments, but will not appear in the profit statement.

> What more needs to be said? Cash planning and control are essential for your business but are not matters for amateurs. Expert assistance should be sought. It is in your interests that you plan and control cash

DEVELOPING VALUE ATTITUDES
TOWARDS RESOURCES

8

All business activity revolves around money. When more money flows into a business than out of it, there will be profits. Knowing how to be entrepreneurial in managing your financial affairs is essential to being profitable in business

You have your business; or perhaps you are planning a new venture. It is natural to plan with physical assets in mind:

☐ People (you have or need). *How will they perform? Are they reliable? Should some be promoted?*

☐ Your business location. *Will it attract the customer? Are services acceptable? What about future expansion?*

☐ Your business layout (whether factory or corner store). *Does it help staff to service customers? Are there bottlenecks? Can it be reorganised?*

Also to be taken into account are buildings, plant, vehicles and inventory. These are essential resources for your success, and the questions about them must be taken seriously. But being *entrepreneurial* requires more.

Business activity involves money. Sales bring in money; expenses commit the business to spending money; success generally is measured through the "bottom line" of the income statement: net profit. Your investment in the business is measured in money. You should therefore see your business resources as cash investments that are working for you and producing a satisfactory financial reward.

As an entrepreneur you want to succeed; you want to be in control of your day-to-day financial affairs; you want to know that the *future* is being looked at carefully, with plans for uncertainties; and that prospects continue to meet your objectives. In other words, you want answers to these questions:

☐ What's my investment now? What are my resources in financial terms?

☐ How do my financial rewards measure up against my investment?

☐ Do I need additional resources? What are the financial implications?

☐ What are the vital factors in keeping my business on the road to success? Can I control these factors day by day?

☐ What of the future? What investment? What resources? What rewards?

☐ Should I seek assistance on financial matters? Where can I get this help?

> Control over day-to-day financial affairs is essential to planning your business activities. Informed responses to the above questions should enable you to understand and control the future of your business

MEASURING YOUR RESOURCES

The physical resources of your business are *assets*. You acquire assets to help to develop your activities and achieve your goals. Assets are *used* to generate sales and hence profits. As an entrepreneur, you will look on *all* assets in this way. You buy inventory to sell at a profit; buildings to use for business; display cases to increase sales; vehicles to save costs or for expansion of your operations.

Some assets are converted into sales, profits and cash relatively quickly. These are *current assets*. Examples are cash, bank balances, inventory (either raw materials, partly manufactured items or merchandise ready for sale); and debtors (or accounts receivable). Other assets are used to support the business and are *not* for sale: for example, vehicles, buildings, land, plant and equipment. These are referred to as *fixed assets*.

Both current and fixed assets are generally measured in terms of *cost* to your business: the invoice cost of inventory, the invoice cost of machinery and plant, the construction cost of buildings, and so on. As an entrepreneur you are interested in the "market" or "current" cost of these resources. What is the replacement cost of the inventory now? What is the replacement cost of the land and buildings you own? This information allows you to make key decisions on pricing, and/or whether to sell your current factory site and move to a new location. As an entrepreneur, you are constantly questioning and planning for the more efficient use of your

Table 1. Measurement of assets

Type of assets	Retail/wholesale firm		Manufacturing firm	
	Cost	Current	Cost	Current
Current	$	$	$	$
Cash	2 000	2 000	2 000	2 000
Bank	8 000	8 000	8 000	8 000
Inventory	16 000	18 000	40 000	60 000
Debtor	9 000	9 000	10 000	9 000
Subtotal	35 000	37 000	60 000	79 000
Fixed				
Land	16 000	30 000	20 000	60 000
Buildings	90 000	120 000	140 000	180 000
Plant	10 000	12 000	80 000	90 000
Vehicles	7 000	8 000	14 000	16 000
Subtotal	123 000	170 000	254 000	346 000
Total	158 000	207 000	314 000	425 000

resources. In terms of purchase cost and current replacement cost, your assets may be measured financially as shown in table 1.

Being entrepreneurial, you will want to ask some questions about the sums recorded under "Cost" and "Current":

☐ If there is a significant difference between the cost and current sums, what is the future trend likely to be? How does this trend affect my objectives for the future?

☐ Are we holding too much cash? Is the bank balance too high? Can the funds be used efficiently elsewhere? Is it idle cash? What happens to the cash/bank balance day by day, week by week, month by month?

☐ Are we carrying too much inventory (most businesses are!)? Can we re-schedule orders to reduce our investment? Will the suppliers deliver to meet *our* needs, not their requirements?

☐ What of the land investment? Do we need the land? Can it be sold? Or is it being held as a hedge against inflation?

As an entrepreneur, you will wish to take a positive attitude towards your resources. For this, you need to know what you control. However, assets are not your only resources. You have access to finance and credit from others in business, and you have your (and other owners') funds in the business. Thus, a complete statement of financial resources or (as it is often called) the *financial position* or *balance sheet* includes details of loans, creditors, mortgages, and owner's capital or equity (see table 2). Liabilities are claims on your business by others, such as a bank overdraft

Table 2: Specimen statement of financial resources

Assets or liabilities	Retail/wholesale firm		Manufacturing firm	
	Cost	Current	Cost	Current
	$	$	$	$
Total assets	158 000	207 000	314 000	425 000
Less liabilities:				
Current				
Bank overdraft	10 000	10 000	10 000	10 000
Creditors	18 000	18 000	30 000	30 000
Subtotal	28 000	28 000	40 000	40 000
Long-term				
Loans	52 000	52 000	104 000	104 000
Total liabilities	80 000	80 000	144 000	144 000
Equals				
Owner's equity	78 000	127 000	170 000	281 000

that has to be met; loans to be repaid; credit received that must be paid. Some are *current liabilities* (payable in the near future) and others are *long-term liabilities* (debts repayable beyond the current period). Both current and long-term liabilities are always shown in "current cash". Because your investment and funds from others (liabilities) are used to acquire assets, the purchase cost of assets always must equal the cost of liabilities and owner's capital or equity.

Purchase cost of assets = liabilities + owner's investment (or equity)

Many questions are raised by the financial statement. Is the balance between assets and liabilities acceptable? How are assets being financed? Is the business financially stable? Are funds available for future development and growth? These and other questions are answered in other chapters. Now let's look at "rewards" for financial investment

---

MEASURING YOUR REWARDS

Your rewards in money come from performance measured in money. In a retail business, you buy and sell; in a manufacturing business, you buy, process and sell. The end result is profit, which is the difference between revenue and expenses. Because you are in business for yourself (as an entrepreneur), you must seek two contributions as your total reward:

☐ a cash reward for time allocated to your business; and

☐ a cash reward for your financial investment—keeping in mind the risk connected with *your* business.

Your cash time reward

How can you measure your time reward? As you would for any employee: base it on hours worked, experience, qualifications and responsibilities accepted:

☐ Hours: How many *effective* hours per day, week, year do you devote to your business? What number could be called "normal" working hours? How many are "overtime"?

☐ Experience: Management? Breadth? Industries? Number of years?

☐ Qualifications: Certificates? Diplomas? Degrees? Trade qualifications? Special management training?

☐ Responsibilities: Staff controlled? Volume of sales? Product areas? Growth of business?

In your case, the starting-point may be a basic salary for a manager in a comparable business. To this basic salary may be added "loadings" for hours worked, experience, qualifications and responsibility. For example:

	$
Basic salary (say)	15 000
Loading:	
Hours worked	2 000
Qualifications	500
Experience	1 500
Responsibility	3 000
Total	22 000

How does this time reward of $22,000 per annum compare with a salary you would expect to pay a manager who took your place, with similar experience, qualifications and responsibilities, and who was prepared to work similar hours? If your assessment is close to the $22,000 figure, you are ready for the next calculation: an entrepreneurial reward for your *business* investment.

Your financial investment reward

You are *entitled* to a reward for your business investment. If you invested money through the stock exchange, you would expect a dividend return from the shares (stock) purchased. If you invested money in bonds or a bank savings account, you would expect a return in the form of interest. Your investment in your business also should give you a return. The size of the return depends on your assessment of business risk: risk for your *industry* and your *business* in the industry.

People have different ideas of what represents "high" and "low" risk. To one person, an investment seen as high risk may need an annual return of (say) 80 per cent to attract money. To another person, a high risk return may be acceptable at 60 per cent; others may require 100 per cent or 200 per cent.

A lower limit can be set for the return from "safe" or "low" risk investments. A return on government bonds may be regarded as low risk; and if the current rate is (say) 10 per cent per annum, this gives us the lower limit since *your business* is unlikely to represent a risk lower than government bonds. Thus, we have a basis on which to assess your risk:

Step 1	*Step 2*	*Step 3*
Your assessment of high and low risk return	*Where is your industry risk?*	*Where is your business risk?*
%	%	%
High 80	High 60	High 50
	Acceptable 40	Acceptable 30
Low 10	Low 15	Low 20

What does it mean? *Your* assessment of risk for your business is that in the early stages of start-up and development (high risk), the return on investment should be about 50 per cent. *Now*, a return of 30 per cent would be acceptable; and as the business grows and becomes well established (low risk), an acceptable return might be as low as 20 per cent.

We now apply this to our retail/wholesale example. The *current* measure of owner's equity (investment) was $127,000, so a return of 30 per cent means $38,100 per annum.

Your total reward

Time reward	22 000
Investment reward	38 100
Total	60 100

This figure is *before* taxation and has to be sufficiently large to allow cash withdrawal (as profits) for personal living; *and* pay your taxes; *and* allow reinvestment into the business for growth and development.

Determining your financial rewards involves two factors: a cash reward for your time; and a cash reward for your financial investment. Calculating your value to the business is a rational means of determining the cash reward of being an entrepreneur

---

CONTROLLING THE CRITICAL FINANCIAL FACTORS

Each business has certain unique features which are critical for short- and long-term success. In retailing, critical financial factors may be gross or net margins, stockturn, overheads, and staff productivity. For a manufacturer, the cost of raw materials or distribution may be critical. In a service industry, labour costs may determine success or failure. Your business strategy as an entrepreneur will be influenced by these critical financial factors. The following illustration is given to emphasise the point. A retail owner may recognise gross margin and stockturn as critical factors to store success. Gross margin is the percentage of gross profit to sales. Stockturn is the relationship between cost of goods actually sold and average inventory held for sale. High margins mean high profits *but* also high prices and perhaps buyer resistance; that is, low stockturn.

Low margins mean lower prices but (perhaps) high stockturn. Thus the "trick of the trade" is to set prices and control stockturn in such a way as to maximise gross profit and—you hope—net profit. A "rule of thumb" often used in the retail trade is:

"Gross margin × stockturn = 135 or more"

Thus	35%	× 4.0	= 140
or	30%	× 4.5	= 135
or	40%	× 3.5	= 140
or	25%	× 5.5	= 137.5
or	20%	× 7.0	= 140
or	10%	× 13.5	= 135

Low-margin operations look for very high stockturns, and the opposite applies for high-margin stores. A furniture retailer therefore can decide (as a strategy) whether to sell top-quality, hand-made, high-margin furniture or to market standardised, low-margin, production-line furniture. The latter will seek high stockturn; the former probably expects low stockturn.

It is important to know the financial implications of alternative strategies. As an entrepreneur, identify your business critical factors *and* the financial impact of the factors on business success

---

FINANCE

An entrepreneural attitude to finance rejects the careless approach to using funds so often characteristic of small business. Studies of business failure in most developed nations have shown that poor financial planning ranks high as a major management "trap". Too many small businesses fail to control liquidity—the equity/debt fund "mix"—to the best advantage: they fail to see finance (money) as a resource to be controlled.

To control finance, you must understand the "finance cycle", linking your initial investment to revenue, expenses, profits, rewards to yourself and reinvested profits. This cycle is illustrated in figure 10.

If you have researched your "business idea", you will by now have invested funds in the enterprise and increased the "pool" of funds. Some of the funds available will be committed to assets, fixed or current. Other funds will meet expenses and generate sales and profits. Profits are your rewards, some to be withdrawn from the business and some to reinvest to build up your investment or equity. Thus, a new group of entrepreneurial strategies emerges:

☐ Should all the equity funds come from *your* pocket? Do you want partners?

☐ Should you borrow? What type of funds? How much? What control could you lose?

☐ Can you use short-term credit? On what terms?

☐ Can the major financial risks be shared? Shifted? Eliminated?

It is self-evident that if you can borrow at 15 per cent and earn 30 per cent on the funds, the result is entrepreneurial success. If your earning rate falls to 12 per cent, the result is misery and disaster.

Finance must be controlled and organised. You must take a positive attitude to fund mix. You will probably require professional advice and guidance

---

Figure 10. Finance cycle

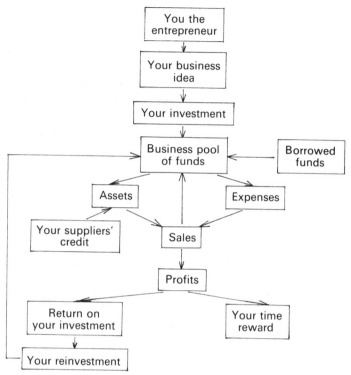

CONTROL AND THE FUTURE

Planning time-spans for the entrepreneur stretch well into the future. Entrepreneurs are prepared for the uncertainties around the corner; are convinced they can "control" the business environment in which they operate; and are ever ready to cope with factors and influences beyond their control with alternative strategies. Your planning should *not* be a fruitless academic exercise but rather a disciplined approach to the future of the business. Planning means thinking through strategies for your business, given an uncertain environment. It is a good discipline to commit facts and figures to paper, checking and rechecking them until you are satisfied that you have a financial plan that is achievable. You will need to make clear decisions on rewards, levels of efficiency, market strategies, cost alternatives, investment, and people productivity. Planning is a challenge, and to meet it you draw on past experience and expert advice in order to shape the future of your business.

The suggested approach and starting-point are appropriate for the entrepreneur: they are positive and aggressive.

☐ Determine the reward to which you are entitled—be positive.

☐ Establish your business efficiency level—be positive.

☐ Given these two factors (cash rewards and efficiency levels), calculate (*a*) sales (revenue); (*b*) expenses; (*c*) investment required; and (*d*) productivity expected/necessary.

☐ Check and recheck; revise and be satisfied with your result.

☐ Communicate with your staff, being enthusiastic and positive.

☐ Control and monitor performance during the planning period.

Details of the planning process are given in the next chapter but the first two steps are illustrated below as an extension of the earlier section "Measuring your rewards", because they are the essence of entrepreneurial attitudes in business.

In that section, rewards for you, the entrepreneur, were divided between a cash time reward ($22,000 in the example); and a cash investment reward (about $38,000 in the example). These gave a total reward of approximately $60,000 for the year. You may recall that these figures were based on realistic factors: time, experience, qualifications, responsibility, financial investment, and risk levels.

Step 2 brings in the efficiency factor. How should efficiency be measured? Some of the appropriate measures for the entrepreneur are discussed in several following pages, but the market-place focuses on one particular ratio: the net margin percentage.

$$\frac{\text{Net profit (before taxation)}}{\text{Sales revenue}} \times \frac{100}{1}\%$$

Net margin percentages vary widely from one industry to another. In the food retail industry, net margins may be as low as 2 or 3 per cent. For specialised, high-quality, low-turnover items, the net margins may be over 50 per cent. Every entrepreneur wishes to improve efficiency (margins), and step 2 in the entrepreneur's planning process is to set efficiency levels for the coming business period. Let us assume you achieved a 9 per cent net margin in your last trading period, and you believe your business should improve this to 10 per cent for the next period (How? We shall see later).

Now we have:

☐ rewards required: $60,000;

☐ efficiency level (margin) required: 10 per cent.

You now know that your business *must* generate sales revenue of $\frac{\$60,000}{10\%}$ or $600,000 for the year.

> Notice again the approach used. Set your reward. Set your business efficiency targets. These facts determine the sales you have to achieve. It is a positive approach—one appropriate for the entrepreneur

Wisdom and getting help

In earlier chapters attention was focused on the entrepreneur's characteristics and attitudes. Now the concern is with the *technical* skills and knowledge of the entrepreneur. Who are the entrepreneurs? Many have experience and technical training in marketing and selling or in engineering and the sciences. *Few* have experience and training in the wide spectrum of management skills and expertise expected of the owner/manager. You will be required to make decisions on finance, reporting, government regulations, legal matters, accounting, organisation, personnel—as well as marketing, buying, selling and production. Very few (if any) entrepreneurs have management experience and expertise in *all* areas. In this chapter, the focus has been on finance, and in this area problems generally arise because:

☐ Few entrepreneurs have any training and experience in financial management.

☐ Many are reluctant to seek expert help and assistance, which leads to financial difficulties, restrictions in growth and development of the business or, even, business failure.

Taking a *positive* stance suggests the following approach:

☐ Attend classes and seminars to gain sufficient background knowledge to allow you to understand basic financial problems and to communicate with the professionals.

☐ Find a qualified professional adviser who is *management*-oriented in his or her approach to finance. You also want a good tax adviser—the management/tax professional may or may not be the same person.

☐ Use the advice given—create an atmosphere which brings the adviser to your business on a regular basis.

> So, you are beginning to be entrepreneurial concerning financial management—getting the "big picture"; being positive in planning and control and getting professional assistance because it is in your interests to do so. The following chapters give more detail on each of these points, starting with financial goal-setting and planning

MEASURING AND CONTROLLING FINANCIAL STRATEGIES AND RESULTS

9

> The previous two chapters emphasised the need to develop money attitudes to your business resources and dealt with the preparation of financial action plans. We now concentrate on the importance of controlling the results of your business endeavours, generating corrective action, and coming to grips with the question of finding and using finance for business growth and development

Initially, it is suggested that you focus on:
- [ ] critical factor control;
- [ ] trends;
- [ ] profit generators;
- [ ] internal and external comparisons; and
- [ ] action meetings.

CRITICAL FACTOR CONTROL

We have already discussed the importance of critical factors in business success for the entrepreneur. No two businesses will necessarily have the same critical factors for success: they are likely to vary from one business sector to another, and location or market circumstances may help to determine which particular factors the entrepreneurial manager has to control. For a retail business, the critical factors might be gross margins and stockturn. For a retail store serving a high-income group the critical factor might be the quality of products offered. In another case, the location of the store might be critical. For example, a food store should have good car-parking facilities and be close to a main road.

The entrepreneurial manager of a factory might believe that his production cost or unit distribution cost is the critical factor in business

Table 3.   Inventory performance report, March 19xx

Inventory group	Gross margin (%)		Stockturn	
	Budget	Actual	Budget	Actual
A	18	17	7.5	7.0
B	24	25	5.4	5.6
C	30	31	4.8	4.5
D	25	26	6.0	6.5
E	18	16	8.6	7.1
F	22	25	7.4	5.5
G	33	35	4.5	4.3
Total store	25	26	6.3	5.8

success. If office or factory space is at a premium, its cost might be critical. In the service industries, labour costs, or the location of a service workshop, might be critical factors determining business success.

Profit performance measurement and control reports should focus on these critical factors. Tables 3 and 4 illustrate some fairly simple control reports dealing with gross margins and stockturn (table 3) and production unit costs—material, labour and overhead components— (table 4).

The entrepreneur is interested in critical factor performance and therefore focuses on margins and stockturn, in terms of both budget targets and actual results. The entrepreneur will expect his managers to analyse the results of product sales for which they are responsible. Thus, if one product group produces a margin of 17 per cent instead of the 18 per cent predicted in the budget, an explanation is required. Even if the margin is higher than that predicted, the difference should be explained as a possible guide to future action. Remember that, as an entrepreneur, you should continually be asking the question: "Why?".

Approach stockturn figures in the same way: results which differ from budget predictions must be explained. The results might be affected over- all by particular activities in certain departments. If, for example, a departmental manager increases the selling price of a big-selling product (thereby increasing gross margins) stockturn could fall and wipe out any extra profit from the price increase. In table 3, Products C, F and G may be examples of this type of result. Product C reported a gross margin of 31 per cent, against a budget expectation of 30 per cent; but the stockturn was lower than expected. The same result was reported for Products F and G. But before any explanation is accepted, the

Table 4.   Production unit cost report, March 19xx (in $)

Inventory group	Material		Labour		Overheads		Total	
	Budget	Actual	Budget	Actual	Budget	Actual	Budget	Actual
A	1.40	1.50	0.40	0.36	0.80	0.72	2.60	2.58
B	3.60	3.40	0.85	0.90	0.70	1.80	5.15	6.10
C	4.25	4.20	1.12	1.15	2.24	2.30	7.61	7.65
D	1.70	1.75	2.36	2.45	4.72	4.90	8.78	9.10
E	2.60	2.55	1.42	1.49	2.84	2.98	6.86	7.02

entrepreneur will expect his department managers to investigate. Some product lines reported lower gross margins *and* lower stockturns than expected, and a thorough investigation of these would be necessary.

Entrepreneurs should expect managers to deal with details while controlling over-all gross margin and stockturn. At first glance, over-all gross margin for the total operation looks acceptable; actual 26 per cent, as against budget 25 per cent. However, this higher gross margin was achieved at the expense of a lower stockturn. In fact, the over-all profitability is lower than budget expectations, so that the higher gross margins were *not* high enough to offset reduced stockturn.

Think of the formula: Gross margin × stockturn   = ????
Budget expectation: 25% ×   6.3   = 157.5
Actual performance: 26% ×   5.8   = 150.8

To offset the higher gross margin achieved, actual stockturn could have fallen to (157.5 ÷ 26%) or 6.06. The actual stockturn of 5.8 was too far below budget to maintain over-all profitability.

Now, let us turn to the report of production unit costs (table 4)— possibly a report for an entrepreneur manager who believes unit cost to be a critical factor in business success. Unit cost is analysed into three components: material, labour and overheads. Budget and actual figures are again reported, together with total unit cost per inventory group. The entrepreneur can maintain over-all control with a total unit cost if this is meaningful; otherwise total unit cost for each product group would serve as the basis for owner control, with individual divisional managers being responsible for each item of cost for each inventory group.

These simple illustrations could be repeated for many critical areas of any particular business. Also, examples could be given that relate specifically to retail, service, wholesale and manufacturing enterprises. As the entrepreneur, you must develop your own set of critical factor reports.

Remember the important principle that reports are to help you to control over-all financial position and performance, to learn from past experience, to eliminate weaknesses, to build on strengths, and to encourage staff to accept responsibilities and make decisions. Keep the report formats *simple*. Focus on key facts. Remember also that preparing and analysing the reports is an exercise in self-discipline. Positive follow-up is crucial

TRENDS

As an entrepreneur, you should focus on critical factors, but you should also be alert to the ways in which changing circumstances may affect your business. Be prepared for problems before they arrive. If costs are beginning to increase, take corrective action *before* your profitability has disappeared. If sales figures for an individual product show that its profits will soon be negligible, you must work out how to put things right.

In Chapter 7 past results were used as a basis for future estimates. The same method can be applied to controlling your operations day by day, week by week, and month by month. Operating reports which reveal trends will help you in this. Table 5 illustrates one report format for product sales for the current period (month, year) and last year. The last two columns are budget figures for last year and for this year. Each of the figures tells a particular story, and should lead to an investigation by yourself or your support staff.

Visual representations of business results are often easier to grasp than mere lists of numbers. In figure 11 the sales results shown could be made even more meaningful if budget expectations were also depicted.

This approach to controlling operations and focusing on trends can be applied to all the critical factors of your business, whether these be unit costs of production, sales, gross margins, labour costs, floor space costs, or any other item

PROFIT GENERATORS

Who or what are your business profit generators? You will be aware that not all sections of your business contribute equally to the final profit line. Some products have higher gross margins than others. Some people are more productive than others. Some plant and machinery produce goods that can be sold at relatively high prices at relatively low

Table 5. Product sales: trend report, March 19xx (in $)

Product	Current year		Last year		Budget	
	This month	Year to date	This month	Year to date	This year	Last year
A	22 430	76 390	21 420	75 900	87 300	85 600
B	10 360	33 190	11 610	34 140	41 200	40 000
C	8 420	21 310	7 430	20 860	31 400	31 000
D	17 410	48 260	16 910	47 690	71 000	70 500
E	6 200	15 180	8 420	16 190	24 300	24 000

production costs. Some store locations mean high profits, while other stores (at poor locations) may be only marginally profitable.

Thus the profit generators of your business may be people, machine, capital, products, locations—in fact, any resource that is available to you as an entrepreneur. If you are interested in analysing the future development of your business, you will want to identify your *real* profit generators. For this reason, your profit control reports may focus on any one of the possible profit generators of your business:

☐ *Product groups.* Obviously seen by many owners as profit generators. Therefore, you should obtain from your business information system facts and figures which tell you which products are most and least profitable.

☐ *Production centres.* As an owner of a factory you may have products passing through several production centres, each with its own costs and productivity performance. If your reports focus on production centres and their performances, you may in fact be focusing on future profits.

☐ *Selling centres.* It is commonplace for managers to produce control reports revealing the revenue generated by, and the costs of, selling centres (which may be separate retail sales outlets or selling divisions within your retail store).

☐ *Cost control centres.* Any business can be divided into cost areas. People are given specific responsibilities for control on the assumption that cost control means profit control. Your business organisation can focus on cost control, from factory costs to administration. It is often one way of getting co-operation from staff who are given special responsibilities.

☐ *People.* Individuals, or groups of staff members, may be seen as profit generators. Business reports would focus on the results achieved by these people: production, selling, buying and administration. These reports may be seen as motivators, particularly when the people

Figure 11. Monthly and cumulative sales

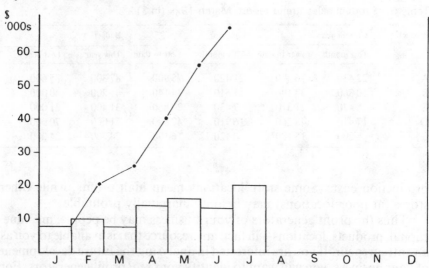

involved also participate in setting standards of performance against which actual performance will be measured.

☐ *Distribution patterns.* Different patterns make different contributions to profits. You may be interested in the contribution of distribution of products through (for example) shipping, air freight, rail and road services to profits. Mail-order versus direct selling may be of interest in your business. As a retailer, you may wish to identify the contribution to profits of counter versus self-service selling, and so on.

☐ *National or international organisational units.* Separate organisational units within one country or across national borders may represent profit generators in your business. Within your country you may organise business units by region or on a country-versus-city basis. Individual branches in various countries may be seen as separate profit-generating units. This approach is a common one for multi-national organisations.

☐ *High-margin services/products.* Separate reports may be justified for both high- and low-margin products or services. As an entrepreneur, you will be looking continually at new approaches to performance analysis; and a simple analysis of product performance as set out in table 6 may be useful to you. What you are interested in is the dependence of your business on high- and low-margin products/services, and to what extent you can shift from low to high margins.

☐ *High productivity groups.* Special reports may act as motivators for your staff. Productivity can be measured in a variety of ways, and the

Table 6. Product gross margins actually achieved

Item	Gross margin (%)						
	Less than 20	20–22	22–25	25–27	27–30	30–35	35–40
Total revenue	18 000	21 000	23 500	20 800	17 500	13 000	8 500
Cost of sales	14 940	16 590	17 860	15 392	12 425	8 580	5 270
Gross margin	3 060	4 410	5 640	5 408	5 075	4 420	3 230

Table 7. Sales per person/group for the month

Item	Amount of sales per person				
	Less than $10,000	$10,000–15,000	$15,000–20,000	$20,000–30,000	$30,000+
No. of persons per group	7	10	6	3	1
Total revenue	56 000	121 000	108 500	77 800	34 500
Cost of sales	45 920	96 800	87 350	61 460	28 120
Gross margin	10 080	24 200	21 150	16 340	6 380

method adopted should suit your own business. One special report could analyse revenue and cost results for staff with "sales per person" performance. This means that your system must be able to record costs and revenues per person. For retail and wholesale stores this is not difficult. Thus, one report could analyse revenue, cost of sales and gross margins as shown in table 7. Naturally, a range of "productivity measures" could be used for a series of reports focusing attention on people and/or capital productivity.

☐ *Low-cost centres.* These could be seen as a variation of productivity centre reports, but they are important because they may serve as examples to the staff. Low-cost centres may be located in a factory, warehouse, administrative unit, service shop or retail unit. Use them to highlight key features of your enterprise.

> Any group or centre in your enterprise can be seen as a profit generator. It is up to you as the entrepreneur to decide what profit generators are appropriate for your business and your objectives

INTERNAL AND EXTERNAL COMPARISONS

Everything that has been said and all the recommendations made so far have assumed that you would be analysing your business and making comparisons from facts and figures available from within your business:

internal comparisons, ratios and trends. You may compare sales this month with sales last month or this month with the same month of the previous year. You may take the same approach with costs and expenses, productivity, returns and rewards. Internal facts and figures for internal comparisons come from within your own accounting system; and you can adjust the system to meet your specific needs.

No entrepreneur should be satisfied with *internal* comparisons alone. Comparing your operations with previous periods may or may not identify all strengths and weaknesses and probably will not give you the satisfaction you would get if you realised that your business was among the "top" performers. As an entrepreneur, you will want to take a long-term view of your business position in the industry. You will be concerned with the position of your business in the industry, not only from an over-all profitability point of view, but also from the point of view of your ranking in sales, margins, individual expenses, returns, productivity, and so on. In other words, you will want internal and *external* comparisons made between your business and the industry on a regular basis. These external comparisons are referred to as "industry comparisons", "industry profiles", "inter-firm comparisons" or "inter-business comparisons".

Hundreds of industry groups in many countries are offering external business comparisons to entrepreneurs. You should find out whether such a scheme is available in your region. If one is not operating in your industry or region at present, you could encourage your industry association or government to organise a scheme as soon as possible. Most comparison schemes operate so that:

☐ Confidentiality of individual business results is guaranteed.

☐ Enough business units in the industry participate to ensure valid comparisons.

☐ Industry norms are in the form of "means" or "averages".

☐ Each participating business receives an individual report comparing its results with industry norms, and ranking the business in the industry.

☐ Analyses are presented for industry units divided into:
  — groups by size, measured in terms of turnover;
  — groups by size, measured as number of personnel;
  — groups by size, measured as capital invested;
  — product/service groups;
  — groups by business location; and
  — any special grouping required by participants.

☐ Comparisons are made at least yearly, and at times every three to six months.

Table 8. Enterprise comparison report: industry comparison scheme[1]

Example: Prepared by University of New England Research Centre, Armidale, New South Wales

Industry: Hardware retail   No. of firms this survey: 326   Your confidential code: 4236

Factors	Your firm result	Average all firms	Your rank in the industry	Average results – Firms by size (Sales volume in $)				
				Up to $50,000 (84 firms)	$50,000 to $200,000 (77 firms)	$200,000 to $500,000 (71 firms)	$500,000 to $1m (53 firms)	$1m + (41 firms)
Financial overview								
Sales this year	$167 400	$703 100	242	$32 100	$135 400	$338 700	$787 000	$2 540 000
Cost of sales	115 500	526 800	75	21 200	93 400	243 900	583 400	1 955 800
Gross profit	41 900	189 800	274	10 900	42 000	94 800	204 600	584 200
Expenses	30 200	119 500	83	4 500	21 700	57 600	141 700	431 800
Net profit (B-tax)	11 700	70 300	268	6 400	20 300	37 200	62 900	152 400
Owners' salary	10 000	34 000	164	8 000	15 000	28 000	32 000	60 000
Return for investment	1 700	36 300	290	1 600	5 300	9 200	30 900	92 400
Relative performance								
Sales growth %	8%	15%	180	9%	12%	20%	22%	24%
Gross profit margin %	25%	27%	197	34%	31%	28%	26%	23%
Expense/sales %	18%	17%	150	14%	16%	17%	18%	17%
Net profit margin %	7%	10%	149	20%	15%	11%	8%	6%
Productivity								
Sales per person	$40 200	$52 000	173	$20 600	$34 000	$58 000	$56 000	$51 000
Sales per $ wages paid	$5.60	$7.20	187	$4.70	$6.80	$7.30	$8.30	$8.80
Gross profit/person	$10 600	$13 600	160	$7 600	$10 500	$15 800	$14 600	$11 700
Gross profit/$ wages paid	$1.40	$1.90	178	$1.60	$2.10	$2.00	$2.20	$2.00

N.B. Other ratios included: assets, return on funds, stock, staff structure, expense details, source of revenue, growth or trends in profits plus special ratios for each industry group.

1 Adapted by permission of the Financial Management Research Centre, University of New England, Armidale, New South Wales (Australia).

☐ A follow-up seminar or conference may be held for participants to discuss the implications for individual enterprises and the industry.

A typical report format for a participant is given in table 8. It illustrates some of the many possible ratios that could be used in external comparisons.

Note the following points about the report:

☐ It identifies the individual business with a code number (4236) to maintain confidentiality.

☐ Factors or ratios used in the comparison are very similar to those we have been looking at in the previous two chapters.

☐ One part of the report shows your results, the average for all firms in the comparison, and your rank in the industry for each item compared: for example, Firm 4326 was ranked 242 in the group of 326 businesses for sales; but 290 in the group for return on investment.

☐ This report illustrates averages for all businesses classified by sales level, but other information could have been presented. Most reports to individual participating firms contain several pages of comparisons.

☐ In most industry comparison schemes, participants agree among themselves what ratios should be used and what format would be most beneficial for decision-making.

The external comparison report is an excellent tool for the entrepreneurial owner. It focuses attention on your strengths and weaknesses, opportunities for improvement, and strategy alternatives.

> External comparison reports can boost your own confidence. They can also motivate staff who would gain from knowing how they perform in comparison with their competitors. Involving your staff in this way will lead to improved productivity and profitability

---

ACTION MEETINGS

What happens when you find that there is a significant difference between your plans and your actual performance? It doesn't matter whether the performance is in terms of sales revenue, plant efficiency, administrative cost control—or whatever! The entrepreneurial answer should be "Action meetings!" To be effective, action meetings must lead to action, feedback and further decisions. An effective method of ensuring that action meetings are controlled (in terms of the time spent on them and of effective results) is to hold meetings only when some specific problem is to be investigated or some feedback on a past action is

Figure 12. Action Report Form

Date	Item	Person responsible	Action	Date to report
12 November	Product "A" Profitability analysis	J. Smith	Review cost and sales	23 November

required. Action meeting *reports* are often a useful means of controlling discussions and getting results. A simple action report form is given in figure 12. In this example, a meeting was held on 12 November because a particular product group was not producing an expected level of profitability. A staff member is given the responsibility of investigating the problem and a line of action is suggested, together with a specific date for a report to be presented.

> A simple action meeting plan ensures that action is carried out; an individual staff member is given and accepts responsibility for a line of action; a deadline is set for future action. Action meetings conducted in this way are positive, well controlled and not too time-consuming, and constitute an exercise in self-discipline

FINANCE STRATEGIES: SOURCES

Earlier, it was stated that finance should be seen as a resource to be managed for the benefit of your business. Ratios also illustrated the operations of financial leverage, such as the use of debt as opposed to equity funds in a business. In other words, when you form your business, you generally expect to provide most of the finance from your own resources. This is your equity capital. As you require additional funds, you will borrow and thus get a mixture of debt and equity funds in the business. Because you generally require a relatively high reward, and therefore a high percentage return on your equity (since you are carrying most of the business risk), the return or reward on equity is always much higher than on the sums borrowed. Thus, you may expect a return of 40 or 50 per cent on your equity funds invested in the business while you may borrow funds as debt capital at a rate of interest of, say, 12 or 15 per cent. Lenders of money to your business will, of course, want some security to reduce their risk.

It is therefore important for you to consider alternative types of available funds, and the sources of funds, if you are going to be entrepreneurial with finance.

Most new enterprises are launched with finance from the savings of the owner and the savings of friends and relations. It may be possible for the new entrepreneur to borrow from a bank as long as some personal assets serve as collateral for the bank. As the business begins its operations, funds will be generated within the business; and other funds may become available from creditors, finance companies, debenture capitalists and government. Thus, we can list the various types and sources of funds which you should consider in your finance strategies:

☐ Equity funds. Your finance in the business which, because it carries most of the risk associated with the business, should attract high returns.

☐ Loans from friends and relations. Some security may or may not be required but a reasonable return for their loans would be expected.

☐ Loans from banking institutions, either by way of a term loan or an overdraft. An overdraft is essentially short-term finance to meet working capital requirements over a few months and should not be used for long-term investment purposes. Term loans from a bank are usually used to purchase fixed assets, such as land, buildings, plant and equipment, for a set period which may vary from bank to bank and country to country.

☐ Trade credit. This can be the cheapest source of finance, especially once you have established a sound, credit-worthy reputation. Being able to carry inventory on account permits your free use of the money involved for 30, 60, 90, 180 or even more days, depending on the arrangements you can make with your suppliers. Remember, credit is based on trust, and trust is only achieved over a period of time through test and trial—so don't let your creditors down and they in turn won't let you down!

☐ Various financial institutions may make available mortgage loans or intermediate-term finance for specific purposes. Usually, these loans are to be used to purchase fixed assets, and security will be required by the lender.

☐ Leasing finance is becoming more and more common and may be used to finance plant, vehicles, equipment, office facilities or even buildings.

☐ Venture capital is often available from special corporations which are prepared to provide funds for a small business venture, initially as a loan, but specifically with the idea of converting the debt capital into equity at some future period. It would be normal for the venture capital corporation to require some say in the management of your business in return for providing venture capital.

☐ In some countries, government finance by way of a direct loan or guarantee loan is available, but conditions vary significantly from one country to another.

> The range of finance available is surprisingly wide, and costs and conditions vary from one type of fund to another. It is important for the entrepreneur to consider all alternatives, seek professional advice (see later), and determine the mix of finance that maximises the potential for the business enterprise

FINANCE STRATEGIES: CONTROLLING INVESTMENT

There is no point in obtaining additional funds from your bank account, friends, relations, government or any private financial institutions unless you are going to use them effectively. Thus, the *investment* of funds is an important aspect of being entrepreneurial with finance.

You should look upon your business as a series of investments rather than one over-all investment. For example, if you have a factory, a warehouse and a retail store outlet, these things represent at least three separate investments—because rather than producing your products for sale, you could purchase the same or similar products direct from another manufacturer or from a wholesale operator. Rather than setting up your own chain of retail stores, you could manufacture your products and sell to a wholesaler or retailer. Each decision is to be a separate investment decision. The same principle applies to *any* business—even a separate factory or a separate retail store. Your factory could partially or completely manufacture your products. Your factory could process its own raw materials or buy raw materials from another operator. Your single retail store is a series of business segments; each segment might represent a different product line *or* a different sales team *or* a different floor space area *or* a different location.

> See your business (whatever it is) as a series of segments, each representing a specific investment

If your business is a series of investments, each must contribute to your total reward; therefore, each segment must earn a reward. The level of the return on each investment will depend on *risk*. Low risk means low returns. High risks suggest high returns. What you must do—being entrepreneurial—is to identify, for each of your business investments, your percentage investment; the risk associated with the investment; financial returns from the investment; and your assessment of the return (acceptable or not acceptable).

It is not difficult for you to ensure that any *new* investments that your business may make will produce an adequate reward for you. What you need to calculate is the cash flow from the new investment, i.e. the amount of cash to be spent to "get the investment off the ground" and the resultant cash inflow once things are operational. And, as an entrepreneur, shouldn't you be interested in the cash flow?

A few simple examples will illustrate the exercise. Assume you were considering the production and sale of a new product for your region. Perhaps the operations will be conducted under a licence granted by an overseas manufacturer. Being entrepreneurial, you will accept that there may be a number of alternative strategies to get your new project off the ground. As often happens, you may have to make a choice, in this case between two alternatives:

(*a*) a relatively low initial investment, low future cash inflows (as revenue), low future cash payments, and hence low future cash surplus, with a relatively short project lifespan; *or*

(*b*) a high initial investment, with appropriate high revenues and expenses, but producing a relatively high future cash surplus for a long period.

These alternatives are illustrated in table 9. Strategy (*a*) is expected to produce annual cash revenue (before taxation) of $10,000, but cash expenses of $7,000 reduce this to a surplus of $3,000 per annum. For this investment return, a cash investment of $9,000 is required and the project is expected to continue as a productive unit for at least ten years.

On the other hand, strategy (*b*) promises an annual cash surplus of $6,000 for a cash investment of $24,000, and has an expected lifespan of 20 years. Is this more attractive than strategy (*a*)? To arrive at a decision the entrepreneur first calculates the "payback period", by dividing the initial cash investment by the annual cash surplus. He then uses this factor to calculate the percentage rate of return on his investment, taking into account the life of the project.

In the two strategies illustrated, you can calculate both the cash payback period and the percentage return on investment, given payback and useful life of projects.

For strategy (*a*) the cash payback period is $9,000/$3,000, or three years. For strategy (*b*) the payback period is $24,000/$6,000, or four

Table 9. Investment alternatives

	Strategy *(a)*	Strategy *(b)*
	$	$
Additional sales per annum	10 000	15 000
Additional cash costs per annum (before taxation)	7 000	9 000
Additional cash surplus per annum	3 000	6 000
Initial cash investment	9 000	24 000
Expected life-span of project	10 years	20 years

Table 10. Return on investment: payback calculator[1]

Useful life-span (years)	Percentage *return* on investment				
5	95	41	20	8	0
10	100	50	31	22	15
15			33	24	18
20				25	19
25					20
30	100	50	33	25	20
	1.0	2.0	3.0	4.0	5.0

Payback period (years)

[1] The figures for percentage return on investment are based on annuity or compound interest calculations which take into account discount factors. Such tables can be found in most accounting textbooks.

years. Using the data in table 10, you can relate these two payback factors to the respective useful life-spans of the strategies to read off the expected return-on-investment percentages.

By relating the cash payback period to the expected useful life-span, you can judge the alternative strategies on percentage return. For example, strategy (a), with its payback of three years and useful life of ten years, indicates a return of 31 per cent. Although strategy (b) expects to continue for 20 years, the payback of four years suggests a return of 25 per cent. Given these facts, it is for you, the entrepreneur, to decide whether the difference in returns is of significance in the decision; and whether other factors are important in the decision.

Incidentally, you may notice that there is a connection between the payback period and the return percentages as life-span increases. For example, projects with a payback of two years *never* produce a return greater than 50 per cent (= 100 per cent ÷ 2). Projects with a payback period of four years *never* produce a percentage return greater than

25 per cent ($= 100$ per cent $\div 4$). Projects with a payback period of five years *never* produce a return percentage greater than 20 per cent ($= 100$ per cent $\div 5$). From this you can make this simple rule:

> When investment projects offer relatively constant annual net cash flows, with life-spans which greatly exceed the payback period, the percentage return on investment is 100 per cent divided by the payback period

Payback period 3 years; lifespan *much greater* than 3 years; percentage return:	$33\frac{1}{3}$
,, ,, 4 ,, ,, ,, ,, 4 ,, ,, ,,	25
,, ,, 8 ,, ,, ,, ,, 8 ,, ,, ,,	$12\frac{1}{2}$
,, ,, 10 ,, ,, ,, ,, 10 ,, ,, ,,	10

and so on.

To take this rule and its application a little further, if you, being entrepreneurial, set a return target for all new investments of (say) 25 per cent, what you are saying is that all new projects should have payback periods of not more than four years and life-spans which far exceed four years.

> You can be entrepreneurial in controlling performance and finance. Performance also depends upon people, and we look at this aspect of being entrepreneurial with finance in the next chapter

FINANCIAL SUCCESS THROUGH PEOPLE   **10**

As an entrepreneur, you should be interested in people because your business success depends on them: your staff, suppliers, customers, advisers, and many others. This chapter shows how the management of people is linked with financial success

No business can succeed under even the most enthusiastic and confident entrepreneur without the full support of employees and others associated with the enterprise. The best product in the world will probably be a failure without an efficient and knowledgeable sales staff. The most efficient equipment in a factory could produce unsaleable products unless competent and dedicated staff supervised and controlled it. People and business success are synonymous. It is important for you as an entrepreneur to recognise that people represent (for your business) an investment. Not only must your machines be productive, but your people must produce effectively and efficiently. The productivity of people can be measured in much the same way as the productivity of plant and equipment. Your staff have rights to fair rewards for their time given to the business: rights based on experience, qualifications, and responsibilities accepted. You, as the entrepreneur, have a right to receive continuing productivity from your staff. Productivity means money; and money means business success and stability.

PEOPLE, INVESTMENT AND RETURNS

When setting up a business, expanding a business, or merely considering possible alternative future strategies, most entrepreneurs have a choice between an operating unit that is either largely "labour-intensive" or "capital-intensive". In other words, the choice is between either hiring additional people, or investing in new capital items such as buildings, plant and equipment. For example, an entrepreneur operating a factory may decide to expand operations, and labour-saving equipment may be installed; or perhaps the entrepreneur may install lower-cost equipment requiring additional staff appointments as well as some capital investment. In the same way, an entrepreneur owning a retail store and wishing to expand operations has to choose between adding more counter facilities (with staff to service the counters) or installing self-service facilities which would require fewer staff appointments.

Most entrepreneurs, believing that they can motivate staff to work positively for the enterprise, will choose the labour-intensive solution to the expansion problem rather than the capital-intensive solution. While this is commendable (particularly in times of unemployment), it is important that you, the entrepreneur, are fully aware of recent increases in labour costs, and of the consequent need to be able to motivate staff sufficiently to increase productivity and profitability.

In recent years, both wages and selling prices have increased while productivity in relation to wages has declined (see figure 13).

Although consumer prices have increased in most countries, wages generally have been increasing at a faster rate than prices, so that "wage productivity" has declined. There are a number of methods for measuring wage productivity and some are illustrated opposite. For our purpose, we can say that the relationship between sales revenue and wages paid is one indicator of wage productivity. It is this type of ratio that has been declining. The result is that larger proportions of profits have been required to pay employees' wages while smaller proportions of profits have been available for owners.

All employees have a *right* to a reward in line with their qualifications and experience, but the entrepreneur also has a right to a fair reward. If this reward is not forthcoming *and* is declining, the enterprise (and its employees) will suffer. Thus, the wage productivity ratios in general should remain constant as product prices and wages costs increase. Being vitally concerned with the financial stability of the enterprise, you should monitor these ratios regularly.

Table 11 illustrates typical cash ratios between people and wage productivity.

Given rises in consumer (product and services) prices, it could be expected that the sales per person would *increase* significantly over the four-year period. But in this example, sales per person have *declined*, suggesting either that the enterprise has too many staff for the level of revenue, or that staff are operating at reduced productivity in terms of sales and profits produced.

The simple solution may *not* be to reduce staff immediately, but to

Figure 13.   Wages, prices and productivity

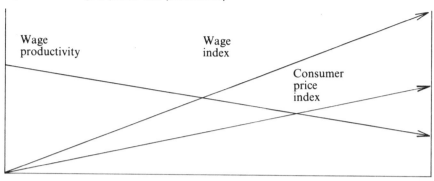

Time

show staff what is happening (part of communication) and discuss with them possible solutions. Perhaps each staff member could be set a target. Senior sales staff might agree that they should sell at least $80,000 per person each year, while junior staff could not be expected to sell more than perhaps $40,000 per year. Allowances must be made for staff experience, opportunities and non-selling duties. Perhaps the standards, or targets, could be set in terms of sales/wages paid. That is, if the staff agree that, on average, a ratio of $10 in sales should be produced for each $1 in wages paid, allowance should be made for experience, so that junior staff are expected to achieve a $8 to $1 ratio, and senior staff a $15 to $1 ratio. Experience has shown that when such standards are used and accepted by staff, productivity increases to the satisfaction of everyone. Being entrepreneurial, you should consider this approach.

There is much to be gained from keeping your staff informed on gross profit margins. Staff must be aware of the relative profitability of products and services, and have some appreciation of the need for the business to achieve a satisfactory product/service/profit "mix". There may be many reasons why some products or services have to be sold at relatively low profit margins. However, we know that if *all* products/services are sold at low margins, turnover must be relatively high to ensure the profitability and stability of the enterprise. A balance is essential, and your staff need to be aware of this balance. Thus, if it is agreed that staff should be aware of gross margins for the enterprise as a whole and for major product/service lines, productivity standards based on gross profit can be set. If, for example, staff are aware that gross profit per person has been declining (as in the example shown in table 11), they will realise that the trend could not be allowed to continue since gross profits have to meet staff wages, business overheads and rewards for

Table 11. People/wage productivity

Ratio	Base year	Year +1	Year +2	Year +3
	$	$	$	$
Sales/person	30 000	29 000	28 000	27 000
Sales/wages paid	9.70	9.00	8.60	8.10
Gross profit/person	9 000	8 700	8 400	8 200
Gross profit/wages paid	2.90	2.65	2.60	2.40

owners. If gross profits are declining, presumably one or more of these three also must decline.

Gross productivity standards can be set by person and by product/service group; and they can be expressed in weekly or even daily terms. For example, let's assume that an employee has a "productivity rate" of $3 gross profit to $1 wages. If his wages are $30 a day, it follows that each day he must sell goods (or services) worth $90 in gross profit.

If daily sales vary during the week, allowances can be made in setting daily productivity ratios. A simple daily sales record system would be necessary to monitor productivity progress, but if it is introduced in a positive and constructive way, staff will welcome the opportunity of measuring their own performances. Being entrepreneurial, you should take the view that staff are prepared to co-operate in the exercise as long as reasonable productivity standards are established.

Now you must apply these examples to your business by adopting the general principles to suit your particular needs, adjusting standards for differences in staff, product, service, and so on, and collecting facts and figures from past financial records to identify *your* business trends. For example, most enterprises have taxation return records available, and these will show sales, gross profits, wages paid and number of people employed. Calculate your ratios for (say) five years, discuss the results with staff and decide what appropriate standards should be set.

> You should include yourself in the ratio calculations and setting of standards if you are at all involved in selling directly. If this is the case, your wage rate too should be included in the ratio calculations. By taking this attitude, you are showing staff that you see productivity as being achieved through people, not through machines

PEOPLE HAVE A TIME COST

Most nations have regulations, often based on ILO Conventions and Recommendations, which establish minimum salaries for staff and minimum employment conditions. While these may vary from country to country, the entrepreneurial philosophy of measuring productivity can be applied in any nation and to any business. Every staff member has a "time cost" which must be recognised, measured, and taken into consideration both before and after the hiring decision has been made. You should be selective in the hiring process (from the point of view of finance and performance) and in the allocation of duties within your business. A task that can be carried out by employees with the experience and qualifications appropriate to someone who commands a rate of $5 an hour should *not* be allocated to employees who are paid $8 an hour. Yet this often happens. Employees are often not managed, not motivated, not allocated to tasks appropriate to their time cost. How often are highly paid people doing "low time cost" tasks? An understanding of staff time costs should help you to allocate employees to appropriate tasks, to the satisfaction of all; and therefore lead to improved financial productivity.

The time cost of each employee depends upon the number of "effective" hours worked each year and the salary and salary-related costs. While hours and salaries vary from place to place, the time cost calculation can be illustrated for you to apply to your business. The following figures show one possible calculation of the number of effective hours worked per year by each employee:

Weeks per year	52
Work days per week	$\times 5$
	260
Less statutory holidays	-10
	$= 250$ days
Less recreation leave	-20
	$= 230$
Less sick leave	-10
	$= 220$
Work hours each day	$\times 7\frac{1}{2}$
Potential work hours per year	$= 1\,650$ hours

These figures assume that:
- [ ] work in your business is restricted to five days each week;
- [ ] workers receive ten days each year for statutory holidays such as Christmas, national remembrance day, etc.;

117

☐ each member of staff is entitled to 20 days each year as recreational leave;

☐ on average, a staff member will be absent from work for ten working days each year on full pay; and

☐ each day, seven-and-a-half hours of work are usual after allowing for lunch and other breaks.

Your own circumstances may require these calculations to be modified before proceeding. Remember that the figures apply to the total hours that are *available* from each employee for productive work. It does not mean that the total of 1,650 hours is necessarily the "effective" number of hours worked. To find the effective selling time, or the effective productive time when employees are working in the factory on machines, requires further adjustments. However, the above figures are an appropriate starting-point in calculating what is often called "base time costs" of employees.

Six calculations are included in table 12, but your business might require more or fewer to cover the salaries involved. Notice that the salary figures include "allowances". Sums for insurance or superannuation, or any other item, payable by you in respect of each employee must be included in the total. In this example, the base cost per hour ranges from $3.03 to $15.15; and this illustrates how important it is to allocate people to the right jobs. It would be ludicrous to have executives (paid $15 an hour) doing work that could be done by a man earning $3 an hour. But that often happens.

Now let's look at the effective cost of staff in terms of money. The principles can be illustrated with an example from a service industry where the owners charge clients on a time cost basis, plus material cost. For this reason it is essential that the owners know the "effective" time cost of all employees. Although employees may be hired mainly to provide services to customers, not *all* their time will be spent in this way. Some of their time will be spent on administration, further training, maintenance, and so on. Thus, only a proportion of total employee time may be spent directly on customer work, or be "chargeable". Also, because we are considering the cost of time and a charge rate for employee time, it is to be expected that *revenue* must come into the calculation. It does! We need to know the required revenue for the business, the effective use of time *and* the base time cost of employees. The calculations are illustrated in tables 13 and 14.

Now let's look at each section of table 13:

☐ *Revenue required.* A calculation made by you, based on your reward requirements and efficiency expectations (we have already looked at this calculation).

Table 12.   Base time cost

Salary and allowances	Base hours	Base time cost
$	$	$
5 000	1 650	3.03
7 500	1 650	4.55
10 000	1 650	6.06
15 000	1 650	9.09
20 000	1 650	12.12
25 000	1 650	15.15

Table 13.   Service industry time charges

Revenue required	Owner/staff salaries	% chargeable to total working hours	Base cost: chargeable hours	Charge rate factor
$	$		$	
50 000	32 000	70	22 400	2.23
100 000	58 000	75	43 500	2.30
200 000	135 000	65	87 750	2.28

☐ *Owner/staff salaries.* Your own salary requirements plus salaries and allowances for your staff.

☐ *Percentage chargeable to total working hours.* Amount of time actually spent on clients' work related to total possible hours of work for you and staff.

☐ *Base cost: chargeable hours.* Calculated by applying the percentage chargeable hour rate to owner/staff salaries.

☐ *Charge rate factor.* The amount by which the base time cost of staff has to be increased because all work time is not chargeable to clients; it is calculated by dividing "revenue required" by "base cost: chargeable hours". For example, when revenue required is $50,000, the charge rate factor is $\frac{\$50,000}{\$22,400} = 2.23$.

Notice that the "Revenue required" figure reflects the over-all efficiency of your business (particularly the net margin percentage); and the "Percentage chargeable to total working hours" reflects the efficiency of your staff and yourself. Entrepreneurs are intensely interested in efficiency, particularly staff efficiency. Most would expect a percentage chargeable to total hours of at least 70 per cent, but this figure varies for different staff groups and from industry to industry. What is your business efficiency percentage in terms of time usage? Three examples are included in table 13 to show the effect of varying revenue, salary levels and efficiency. Now make your business calculations. If you do not have dependable statistics on time efficiency, use varying estimates. For example, if your expected revenue requirements were $300,000, and salaries (including your own) totalled $120,000, make your calculations assuming percentages chargeable to total time of (say), 65, 70, 75, 80 and 85 per cent. You will notice that the charge rate factor decreases as time usage increases.

Once you have calculated your charge rate factor for your business in the forthcoming trading period, you can apply this factor to the base time costs (for differing salary rates see table 12) to give you rates to charge clients. Thus if your charge rate factor is 2.30, this factor is applied to various base rates. At $5,000 salary, we found that the base cost was $3.03 an hour, so that the client charge rate is (2.30 × $3.03) = $6.969, or $7 an hour. Charge rates for other salary levels are illustrated in table 14 (these figures are illustrative only).

In table 14 the charge rates for clients vary from $7 an hour for staff commanding an annual salary of $5,000 to $35 an hour for staff commanding an annual salary of $25,000.

Thus, if the above charge rates for client work were used; if the demand for client work meant that 75 per cent of staff time was absorbed in direct client work; and if salary levels and business efficiency factors remained as planned; *then*, the revenue expected would be generated and profits earned.

Even if your business is not in the service industry, you, as entrepreneur, should discover from these calculations the real cost of your own and staff time. Thus, a retailer could calculate the real cost of sales staff selling time by estimating the percentage of time devoted to selling as opposed to administration, buying, reorganising stock, and so on. It all helps you to see how you can control financial performance through people

---

ASSISTANCE AND YOUR ADVISORY BOARD

Being entrepreneurial, you will recognise the importance of continually identifying your strengths and weaknesses, improving your financial and non-financial position, being prepared to reorganise your enterprise, having a positive attitude toward the future, and at all times displaying

Table 14. Charge rates: service industry

Base time cost		Charge rate factor	Charge rates to clients
Salary	Base cost		
$	$		$
5 000	3.03		7
7 500	4.55		11
10 000	6.06		14
15 000	9.09	2.30	21
20 000	12.12		28
25 000	15.15		35

complete confidence in your business and its progress. This theme flows through this book. In addition, there are specific recommendations that from time to time you should seek assistance and advice from external professionals. These professionals may belong to professional bodies, such as accountants, lawyers, consultants, systems analysts and bankers; or the term "professionals" may be taken in a broader context and include fellow entrepreneurs, industry leaders, government officials; in fact, any individual or group capable of contributing to your business growth and development.

It is recommended that entrepreneurs go further than merely using external professionals in the traditional role of consultants. This recommendation is made in the knowledge that while personnel time is a cost to your business, the benefits from sound professional advice specific to your business far exceed the cost.

Your business therefore must have regular access to:

☐ a qualified accountant who takes a "management" view of financial matters;

☐ a qualified solicitor who is prepared to advise on your business legal problems, both those your business faces now and those that may be met in the future;

☐ a management consultant with expertise in the technical field in which you operate;

☐ a banker who appreciates the needs of finance for aggressive business development; and

☐ an "Advisory Board" composed of a small number of specialists— perhaps the four groups set out above (see figure 14).

The use of an Advisory Board requires further explanation and

Figure 14. Your Advisory Board

Consultant/   Accountant/
Technical adviser . . . . Financial adviser

YOU
THE ENTREPRENEUR

Banker/finance   Solicitor/
Investment adviser . . . . Legal adviser

justification. You, as an entrepreneur, have to make key decisions on all aspects of your business management without the assistance of full-time specialists on your staff. Your business may employ a bookkeeper, but you also need a professionally qualified accountant with an awareness of your particular activities and problems. It is unlikely that you will have on your staff an expert in law or finance. What is recommended therefore is a small team of advisers who would meet regularly—for example, once each month—to review plans and financial and non-financial performance; consider alternative strategies; and generally take part in the decision-making process. Even if the monthly meeting of your Advisory Board lasted only two or three hours, there would be some direct and indirect costs with such a system. But if the right people were present the benefits would far exceed the costs.

The Advisory Board plus the professionals with a management outlook whom you consult make an excellent combination of people for you and your staff to work with, so as to ensure that your business is stable and a financial success. But:

☐ Take time and care in selecting your Advisory Board. The individuals must be prepared to allocate time to your business and must become a decision-making team.

☐ Don't allow decisions of the Advisory Board to conflict with advice from professionals. Each has his or her position and job, and you must set guidelines for each. It is possible that some members of your Advisory Board may be your professional advisers; if this is so, see that each understands his or her individual role in each position.

☐ Prepare for each Advisory Board meeting: it is a working, decision-making group, not a social gathering.

☐ Be prepared to pay for productive Advisory Board members; their time is as valuable as yours.

☐ At least once a year, review the activities of the Advisory Board with its members; be objective in assessing its achievements and advantages to you. If it doesn't seem to be working, establish whether the fault lies with you or with the Board members.

> People produce your money. Recognise the importance of staff, customers, suppliers, your professionals and your Advisory Board. In doing so, you are being entrepreneurial

TOOLS FOR CONTROL AND DECISIONS: INFORMATION SYSTEMS

11

> You must keep your employees informed, get them involved, and motivate them with performance standards. Information is the key, and information flow means having reliable systems

Your business success depends on the use of resources: money, clients, physical assets, customers, professional advisers, and your time. The management process that you, as an entrepreneur, follow will include the development of ideas and strategies, the management of people and the administration of systems to ensure that your business flourishes. The development of ideas and strategies, as well as the involvement of people, requires facts and figures.

It is important that you understand how financial and non-financial information has to be collected, analysed, stored, and reported to you and other decision-makers who help the business to succeed.[1] This chapter focuses on the types of information you need as an entrepreneur; on the various reports that you need on a day-by-day, week-by-week and month-by-month basis; and on the development of your systems to keep pace with your business growth.

THE IMPORTANCE OF FACTS

Each year in many nations, business failures are analysed and the reasons for failure identified wherever possible. For example, in the United States the internationally known Dun and Bradstreet organisation regularly analyses failure in that country, and it finds that each year

---

[1] See ILO: *How to read a balance sheet* (Geneva, 12th impr., 1980).

almost 80 per cent of failures appear to be due to managers of businesses being "trapped" in unfavourable positions. These situations would probably not have arisen if satisfactory information systems had been feeding management with relevant facts and figures. For example, many businesses were reported to have failed because their sales were too low. In such cases the business information system may not have reported the failure of sales to meet expectations. It is surprising how many owners do not know from day to day or from week to week the actual sales position of the business.

Other companies reported failure due to excessively high operating expenses. Could this be due to the fact that the information systems failed to accumulate expenses as they occurred, and failed to report actual expenses to management? Other businesses failed because of their poor collection policies. They made the sales, but couldn't collect the cash. Perhaps their information system failed to report credit sales, levels of debtors, ageing of debtors, and the flow of cash from debtors. Also, if cash was not being received from debtors, it might have to be obtained from another source. This would put a burden of additional interest on the company, and could contribute to eventual failure.

Sound and efficient information systems could have saved many of these failed businesses.

Many other businesses failed because too much capital had been tied up in stocks or physical assets. No business can afford to have too much cash in the form of excessive stocks or assets. It means that more cash might have to be borrowed at high interest rates, thus reducing the competitive position of the enterprise. The information system should monitor stock, as well as other physical asset investments and the return on these investments.

In brief, information is vital for business survival; but it is also vital for growth and development. Statistics from the United States emphasise that *lack of information* can lead to overspending or over-investment in assets. Entrepreneurs must have information on which to base their future strategies. The more complex the business, the more important is the information system. An unprofitable strategy (a poor investment strategy) may directly or indirectly lead to business failure. Thus, the information you are looking for includes:

☐ facts and figures for your business strategies that will enable you to make decisions on expansion, construction, additions to products or outlets, additions to factories or warehouses, and so on;

☐ information on your present financial position and obligations to external organisations, such as the amounts due to suppliers of goods and services, the amounts due to lenders of funds, the amounts invested by owners;

☐ information to help you, as the entrepreneur, to control the day-to-day operations of the business, such as cash receipts and payments, balances, sales, balances due to creditors, expenses, profits, actual results compared with prepared plans. You not only want the over-all picture; you also want the information system to provide you and your staff with an analysis by product/division/group/retail outlet, and so on; this is management information in the true sense of the term.

☐ information on the total investment in your business, and investment by division/asset/group, and so on. How much is invested in buildings? Vehicles? Stocks? Debtors? Cash? The system should highlight trends in investment as well as trends in profits;

☐ information on people, including the basic information required by law such as salaries and wages; information allowing you to identify the real costs of hiring and training key staff; information on people productivity and people investment.

Mention was made in a previous section on the importance of comparisons, both internal and external. Your information system should automatically provide you with internal comparisons, such as this month with last month, and probably with the same month last year. This might well be done weekly, monthly and quarterly. It should be possible to feed key industry statistics into your information system so that external comparisons can be made.

> As an entrepreneur, you should be vitally concerned with your information system: its quality; its ability to provide you and your staff with information in a form you want, when you need it; and its ability to develop and adjust to your needs as the business grows

YOUR MANAGEMENT REPORTS

A great deal has already been said or implied about the types of management reports that should flow from your information system. Certain types of reports should be available to you on a daily, monthly, quarterly and annual basis. Many entrepreneurs assume that the information needed for management can be obtained from the returns prepared for government and taxation authorities once a year. This is not so; and you, being entrepreneurial, will see the folly of relying on such annual reports.

Daily/weekly reports

The daily information you require is strictly operational. The facts and figures to meet your day-to-day requirements include: daily cash position; sales summaries (both cash and credit); cash payments; cash received from debtors; cash deposits in bank accounts; and closing cash balances. A simple form that could be used for this purpose is illustrated in figure 15.

This form provides a simple system where cash balances are available at the beginning and the end of each day and can be reconciled with actual cash in the register. One form could be located with each cash register in your business, or all cash transactions could be centralised in one place in the business.

Don't be satisfied with *total* daily sales. Have sales analysed by product group *and* make an estimate of gross profit by product group, given estimated gross margins. The discussion on break-even analysis suggested that the daily cost of being in business could be related to daily gross profit estimates to indicate when (during each week) your business breaks even. Thus, your system should provide daily gross margin estimates and an estimate of the daily cost of being in business; this will allow you to see how you break even and produce profit on a day-by-day basis. The form reproduced as figure 16 could be used to analyse day-by-day sales and margins with each member of the sales staff having a separate form.

From this information you can estimate daily profits or losses, and these can be accumulated day by day to indicate estimated weekly profits (losses). It can be expected that some trading days will produce losses while others will result in high trading profits. The main point is that you are "on top of" the trading facts, and can adjust your trading and cash flow strategy when necessary.

The progressive entrepreneur will also want daily details of inventory so that stock levels are controlled in relation to sales and cash flows. It has already been pointed out that many business failures are caused by poor inventory control. Standard inventory systems are available from consultants and equipment suppliers, and you should find a system that satisfies your business needs.

Monthly reports

On a monthly basis your business should have available:
☐ a detailed profit-and-loss statement;
☐ an analysis of sales and inventory by product/service groups;

Figure 15. Daily/weekly cash flow summary

Day	Date	Opening balance $	Cash received			Cash payments $	Details $	Bank deposits $	Closing balance $
			Cash sales $	Previous credit sales $	Other $				
Sunday									
Monday									
Tuesday									
Wednesday									
Thursday									
Friday									
Saturday									

Figure 16. Sales and profit margin analysis

Day	Date	Product group A			Product group B			Product group C			Total		
		Sales	G.M. %	G.M.$	Sales	G.M. %	G.M.$	Sales	G.M. %	G.M.$	Sales	G.M. %	G.M.$
Sunday													
Monday													
Tuesday													
Wednesday													
Thursday													
Friday													
Saturday													

G.M. = gross margin.

☐ an analysis of cash flow, debtors, creditors and financial commitments; and

☐ an internal ratio analysis revealing efficiency ratings and highlighting trends, with a comparison between your plans and your actual achievements.

This information would coincide with the meeting of your advisory board, the group that joins you in decision-making and strategy development.

Quarterly reports

Naturally, the monthly reports would be available each quarter; but, in addition, the following information should be available for you and your Advisory Board:

☐ a detailed statement of your financial position;

☐ internal and external industry comparisons as measures of efficiency;

☐ trend analyses in more detail than would be prepared for each month; and

☐ information about your current business plant to allow you and your Advisory Board to review activities and project future plans.

Annual reports

The major annual reports are the balance sheet, the profit-and-loss statement and the cash flow statement, which together with the composite quarterly reports provide the basis for strategic planning.

> You, the entrepreneur, must have a reliable information system because without a regular supply of facts and figures you are severely handicapped and are likely to make wrong decisions. The information systems in your business deserve your close attention

SYSTEMS TO MATCH BUSINESS GROWTH

Great strides have been made in recent years in developing sophisticated information systems for specific sectors of industry; and this rapid development of such a wide range of systems has created doubt and confusion in the minds of many entrepreneurs. If considering making a change, you should follow these guidelines:

☐ Seek initial advice from your advisory group, industry associates,

Figure 17. Data-processing alternatives

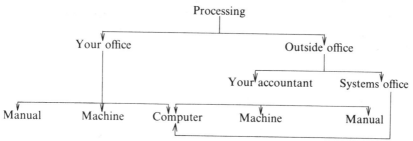

government, small business agencies, professional accountant or consultant, and any other group that can give background information about information systems for your business, industry and location.

☐ Discuss your information requirements with equipment suppliers and systems specialists without making any commitments. Be specific—which requires that you do the initial homework. What do you want the system to do for you and your business team? Document your needs carefully.

☐ Inspect systems in operation in businesses similar to yours. Don't forget that it is important for you to see systems actually in operation. Talk to the owners of those businesses. Are they satisfied with the system? What are the system's strengths? What are the weaknesses? How could it be improved? It is very important to be specific.

☐ Before committing your business to any system, seek further advice from specialists in the field and obtain guarantees from the intended supplier. These would relate to the introduction of the system, the training of staff, and so on.

The various decision options on processing data that are open to you are illustrated in figure 17. You have to process data in some form and at some location. Your basic decision on processing is whether to process within your own business or in some other location. The other location could be an accountant's office or through a data-processing bureau. More and more small data-processing centres or bureaux are being set up to process data for small and medium-sized businesses. Some bureaux specialise in various industry groups and may be in a position to cover your weekly and monthly reports. For these reasons, it is essential that you seek advice from the groups mentioned above to allow you to make the right decisions.

The choice of location must be made with the *method* of processing in mind. There are three basic alternatives: the use of manual systems; the use of non-electric machines; and the use of computers of some kind. Related to these options are questions of capital investment in equipment (or the leasing of equipment); physical space required for equipment; hiring and training of staff; and the methods available to upgrade systems and staff.

Factors which might influence your final decision include:

☐ the size and complexity of the business;

☐ growth and development expectations;

☐ service facilities available for various system installations in your local region;

☐ the quality and quantity of staff available for various system types, and the training facilities available to staff so that systems can be upgraded;

☐ the volume of transactions to be processed; and

☐ financial factors.

Contrary to much that is written and said about systems, most entrepreneurs can obtain adequate and timely information for management decision-making from a manually operated system. On the other hand, it is a fact that mini-computers are becoming available in increasing numbers, and specific systems for industry sectors are available for you and your business. These so-called "management information packages" can often be purchased with the equipment, and may not require any or much modification to suit your specific needs. Another option open to you is to combine manual and computer systems, where internal manual systems give you day-to-day facts which are further processed and analysed by a computer for monthly and quarterly reports and analyses.

All this adds up to the importance of advice from specialists and experienced operators in your industry. Failure to obtain that advice initially might severely limit the ability of your system to expand with business development. It does not make sense for you to give careful attention to the planning, control and financial aspects of your business only to find that major problems arise because you and your colleagues lack the appropriate information to make decisions and control operations.

> Information should be the basis for all decisions. The more complex your business becomes, the greater is your need to develop a foolproof system for gathering information

USING RESOURCES

Part III deals with the use of resources, both within and outside your business. You cannot do everything yourself, and you will depend on people and other resources to help you to become more successful.

Part III includes:
12. Commanding scarce resources
13. Perceiving market opportunities
14. Marketing the product or service
15. Using outside resources
16. Dealing with government agencies

Entrepreneurs must know how to use the resources within their environment to assist them in their entrepreneurial activities. There are many such resources available to entrepreneurs, both within and outside their businesses. Two scarce resources within any business are people and money. Good business planning is necessary to find and keep good employees and to locate money to expand and maintain your business.

Entrepreneurs must be able to develop market opportunities within their environment. Factors leading to new marketing opportunities include conducting market research; gathering data from various sources; and selecting a business location.

Marketing your product or service is another important aspect of business. No matter how good you are in all aspects of operating a business, you cannot be successful unless you are able to sell your products or services. Your business success is determined by customer demand.

There are many resources available to you outside your business. Much of this information is free, but you must be able to know where to look for it. Whenever you do have to pay for outside assistance, make sure that such help is worth the cost. As your business grows, you will have more dealings with various government agencies. These government agencies regulate, monitor and provide assistance to small businesses. Knowing your legal rights and responsibilities will help you to maximise your benefits and minimise your obligations.

COMMANDING SCARCE RESOURCES

12

People and money are two primary resources that are usually in short supply. Finding and keeping good employees is essential to your success. Finding money for the initiation or expansion of your business can be made easier by using a comprehensive business plan

LOCATING PERSONNEL

Employees are an important asset in any business, and your success will depend on relatively few employees. If your business is small, all your employees may be considered key personnel. Employees are important because it is through their efforts that you achieve your goals.

Selecting key employees is one of your most important tasks as an entrepreneur. You may have employees within your business who have the potential for leadership. It is a good policy to promote from within because this provides motivation for your employees to do good work. Giving employees additional responsibilities, in addition to their current duties, is called "job enlargement" and is a good procedure to determine the capabilities of employees to assume higher-level responsibilities.

Outside your business there are many people who could become your key employees. These include—apart from graduates of educational institutions—key employees in competing firms, firms in other industries, and organisations in the public sector.

Graduate business students will have the educational background, motivation and interest to become key employees, but their business experience may be limited. More and more graduate business students are seeking employment in small businesses because they will have more opportunities to be involved in *all* aspects of the operations of a business. This broad learning experience is usually not available in large corporations. When interviewing business graduates, you should stress the career benefits of working in a small firm.

Personnel for top management can often be attracted from your competitors. Because they work in the same type of industry, they will be familiar with most procedures and operations of your business; and they can be expected to be productive from the first day of employment.

Key personnel can also be found in industries unrelated to your own. It will, of course, be important for you to assess whether such a candidate will be able to adapt his general knowledge and skills to your particular business; but a good manager is likely to possess the skills required in most types of businesses.

Finally, potential employees can also be found in public or government organisations. In virtually all countries there are experienced people in government positions who have top management ability.

When looking outside the firm for key employees, try to match the capabilities of the person to the job requirements as much as possible. Locating key personnel may be costly, but it should bring good results.

The following sources should be used when seeking new employees at all levels:

- [ ] employment agencies;
- [ ] recommendations from current and former employees;
- [ ] applications from interested persons;
- [ ] trade unions;
- [ ] all types of educational institutions; and
- [ ] advertisements in papers and magazines.

Communicate your employment needs widely because you never know where or when you will come in contact with potential employees with outstanding abilities. The more candidates you have to choose from, the better your selection should be.

When interviewing a prospective employee, the following questions should help you to evaluate the candidate's potential:

- [ ] What past experience do you feel will benefit you for this job?
- [ ] What are your three major strengths?
- [ ] What are your three major weaknesses?
- [ ] What evidence can you give to illustrate your competence?
- [ ] Why do you want to change your job and join our firm?
- [ ] What are the names of three persons who can serve as referees?
- [ ] Are you willing to take a physical examination?
- [ ] What other information can you give to help us to evaluate your qualifications for this appointment?

Prepare a long list of questions in order to find out as much as possible about each candidate. After you have hired a person, make sure to do everything possible to help him or her to become adjusted to the job.

> Hiring personnel for your firm is an important activity. Spend as much time as possible on selecting the best candidates. They are the people who will contribute most to your success

USING TRAINING RESOURCES

The success of your business is determined by the performance and effectiveness of your employees. Be concerned about the abilities of the people you hire, including their training, experience and motivation. You must also be concerned with the training and development of employees once they are on your staff.

Many outside programmes are available to train your employees. When it is too costly to train the person within your business, outside assistance will be necessary. When considering the benefits of an outside training programme, ask yourself the following questions:

- ☐ Are the objectives of the training programme attuned to my training needs?
- ☐ Do my employees have the necessary background and experience to benefit from the training programme?
- ☐ How will the outcomes of the programme be measured?
- ☐ How will the outcomes be useful to the trainees on their jobs?

Using outside resources to help to improve the skills and abilities of your employees should result in higher productivity; better job performance; higher morale; and reduced staff turnover.

> If your employees improve their efficiency as a result of training, your business will benefit. Knowing when, where and how to use outside training programmes are important questions for you to answer

SUPPLIERS

A business is in a unique situation because it must buy equipment, supplies and materials in one market, and sell its products in another market (see figure 18). To ensure that your business operations run

Figure 18. Business flow

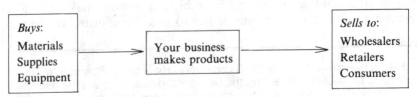

smoothly, you must maintain good relationships with people in both markets.

You must be able to purchase materials in quantities that will ensure that your business can produce goods and services continuously and profitably. The flow of business activity should be smooth and without interruption.

A change in the costs of materials will result in a change of either profits or price. In many instances, various businesses compete for certain

Costs + Profits = Price

materials. Businesses that purchase materials in large quantities may receive special attention and discounts from suppliers. If there is a shortage of materials, the small businesses usually suffer first. Because materials are vital to your success, you must maintain good relations with your suppliers. Be quick to react to changes in the availability of materials, and gather information about future trends which will affect your materials supply.

Most people believe that businesses compete only for the *sale* of products and services. However, there is also competition for the *purchase* of materials to make the products and provide the services. You should constantly seek dependable sources of materials for supplying your needs. To be competitive, you must be just as good at buying as you are at selling.

One of the best methods for developing good relationships with suppliers is for you to promote good communications. Know suppliers on a personal and first-name basis. When materials are in short supply, your goodwill with suppliers will help you to get your orders filled when other businesses may have problems.

Try to have two or more suppliers for items that are not in short supply. If suppliers know that you might buy from others, they will be more likely to give you good service and prompt delivery at reasonable prices. Keep in contact with suppliers; they are an excellent source of information about your competitors concerning prices, products, problems and new technology.

Show suppliers the positive aspects of your business; you probably purchase supplies and materials on credit, and the more positive suppliers are about your business, the more credit you are likely to receive. The more your business operates on credit, the better your financial position will be.

Suppliers should keep you informed of new product development. Using improved materials and components will make your products more attractive to your customers.

If a component of your product represents a large cost, determine the feasibility of making it yourself. For example, if you own a laundry you might consider making your own soap. The lower cost of soap would put you in a better competitive position. If your costs decrease, so can your prices to your customers. A decision to produce soap may allow you to have better control over quality and availability as well as reduced costs. Before committing your firm's resources to producing something you now purchase from suppliers, ask yourself the following questions:

☐ What materials represent a large and continuous cost of conducting business?

☐ How reliable are suppliers who provide you with vital items?

☐ What is the future availability of these items?

☐ Will the savings from producing your own material be worth the effort?

☐ Do you have the resources to accomplish this type of activity?

> Dependable sources of supplies and materials are vital, so maintain good relations with your suppliers. If you have problems with obtaining specific materials, consider making them yourself

---

TECHNOLOGY

Technology is constantly changing the demands of consumers. Business uses new technological developments to produce new products and services, and entrepreneurs should realise that new technological developments will affect the operation of their businesses. You cannot be aware of the nature and effects of all new technologies. Therefore, you must determine the technical developments which are likely to have the greatest impact on your business objectives.

Small businesses are flexible and can innovate and introduce new products. Conversely, small businesses may not have the expertise, time or capital to develop and market a new product. A small business must be realistic in judging demand for a new product; it must also be aware of the financial aspects of developing a new market, as well as the time required to do so.

When considering the introduction of a new product, take into account the developmental time because:

- [ ] it usually takes longer to develop a market than originally planned;
- [ ] the personnel, resources and capital required to market a product may be beyond the capacity of the business;
- [ ] the costs of developing a market are usually higher than expected; and
- [ ] initial success may attract larger companies to enter the market with similar products.

Smaller companies must develop markets where they have a chance to succeed and be competitive.

Because of a shortage of capital resources, you must be able to react quickly to changes in the market and be concerned with the future needs of your customers. Through planning and forecasting you will be able to predict some technological changes that might affect sales of current products and the potential for developing new products. Developing new technologies implies a long-term commitment of resources which most small businesses do not have. Because of day-to-day operating problems, you probably have little time to do long-range planning, even though new technologies will have great impact on your business in the future.

The extent to which your company could be involved in introducing new technology can be determined by answers to such questions as:

- [ ] How will technology affect your company's position in the industry?
- [ ] How will technology affect your profits over the short term and the long term?
- [ ] To what extent are you and your staff currently involved in developing new technologies?
- [ ] How large do you want your business to be in the next five to ten years; and to what extent will technology affect the future size of your business?
- [ ] What growth rate do you want for your business in terms of personnel, markets, and so on; and how will new technology affect your growth rate?

> Your dependence on technology is determined by the environment in which your business operates, and your success may depend on technology relating to: (a) the product itself; (b) your manufacturing method; and (c) your marketing strategies. Your adoption of new technology will also be influenced by the nature and aggressiveness of your competition, the size of the total industry, and its growth rate

Sources of information on new technology

Trade shows usually include new products and new business developments. These trade shows should stimulate your thinking about your firm's future and how these new products might affect your business operations. Trade shows allow you to talk to experts and receive up-to-date information about new products and developments in your area of interest. Looking at developments in other industries can give you ideas as to product trends which may have an impact on your business.

Being a member of a trade association will give you access to publications, special reports and advice about new technology. Read publications from related trade associations because ideas from other trade associations can be applied to your industry.

Some popular periodicals that provide information on new products and new technology are *Popular Science, Popular Mechanics, Wireless World, Flight, Habitation, Micro-systems, Decoration, Elektor* and *Consumer Reports*. These and other publications should help you to generate new ideas. Study the market for new products, emerging trends and changing styles. Your ability to synthesise market information will help to assure your future success.

> New technology may be an important influence in your industry. Be aware of innovations which will benefit your firm in the future

SEEKING FINANCIAL RESOURCES

At one time or another, all small businesses have a need to obtain outside funds. Because financing is so crucial to the initiation and expansion of a business, the rest of this chapter is devoted to this topic.

Your need to borrow

Develop a long-range plan for borrowing that is based on your need for funds for specific purposes, such as trade credit, and short- and long-term credit (see below). Determining the specific use for funds will prevent you from using funds for other purposes. Using operating funds for long-term purposes will eventually require short-term borrowing, and permanent funds may be required to remedy this situation.

Many lending institutions believe that past records reflect the quality of a firm's management. The extent of your success will be found in your profit-and-loss statement. Sales, promotion, expenses, merchandise turnover and net profit are achievements on which you can be judged by a lender.

> Don't create additional problems by borrowing *after* you get into in a financial crisis and need cash immediately. Interest rates will be high and terms for repayment will be unfavourable. Develop a long-range plan for borrowing

Types of money

Most businesses have a need for four basic types of money:

☐ *Trade credit.* This type of money is not really borrowed; rather, it is money you owe your suppliers who allow you to carry inventory on account. Try to pay your suppliers on time. Good credit experience is evidence of your ability to pay your debts. The bank or other lending institution will probably check with some of your suppliers to see if you pay your bills promptly.

☐ *Short-term credit.* Lending institutions provide this type of credit to help you to make purchases for special reasons, such as buying bulk quantities of inventory at a discount. Such loans are self-liquidating because they are designed to produce immediate turnover. Short-term credit is usually repaid within a year.

☐ *Long-term credit.* This type of credit is given for more than a year and may be used for the expansion or modernisation of your business. These loans are repaid from accumulated profits. For small businesses, this type of loan may be a mortgage or a promissory note with special terms.

☐ *Equity funds.* This type of money is not a loan but is obtained by selling an interest in your business to others. These investors share in the profits of a business in return for your use of their money.

Money borrowed for a short-term purpose should be used in the profit-producing areas of your business, and should be repaid from sales.

Equity funds are a part of the business and increase its net worth. Make sure you have sufficient cash to meet your firm's obligations, and that the cash needed for working capital is not being absorbed by your business in other areas of equity and thereby reducing liquidity.

What questions will you be asked?

Your ability to borrow funds when you need them is an important asset. Your lender is more willing to loan you money if your business is profitable, is financially stable, and has growth potential. He will require information about sales, accounts receivable, profits, inventories, fixed assets, short-term obligations, long-term obligations, and other financial information for the past two or three years. Be sure to make these financial data available.

Lenders will probably ask you the following types of questions about the financing of your business. You should give truthful responses and provide proof to support your answers.

Sales

☐ What were your sales figures for last year?
☐ What effects will this loan have on your sales during the next year?
☐ How will projected sales affect profits?

Accounts receivable

☐ What have been your total accounts receivable during the past 12 months?
☐ Why have your accounts receivable increased or decreased during the past year?
☐ What percentage of your sales is on account?
☐ What percentage of accounts are overdue: Two months? Three months? More than three months?
☐ What steps do you take to collect unpaid accounts?

Profits

☐ What is your break-even point?
☐ What has been your profit margin during the past year?
☐ How could you increase your profit margin?
☐ In what ways could you reduce costs and increase profits?
☐ How will market expansion affect your profit margin?

Loan repayment

☐ Is your projected income statement based on past experience?

☐ Is your repayment schedule realistic?

Be prepared to answer these and other questions about your business operations.

How will you repay the loan?

A loan may be denied because the potential borrower was not careful in preparing the loan application. The loan application represents *you*, and it should be logical, clearly stated and well organised. This will indicate to the lender that you have a definite future plan, that you know how much money you need to borrow and are able to justify your cash needs, and that you have a realistic plan to repay the loan.

Choose your lender carefully. Your lending institution should have a reputation for being interested in small business investment. Establish the best possible relations with your lender as early as you can; this involves giving full details of your operation so that he is able to assess your credit status, net worth and over-all business potential. As soon as you have a small need for additional funds, start borrowing and then repay the loan before it is due. It is important to develop a track record which suggests your ability as a manager and your integrity and reliability in repaying debts when or before they are due. As part of a borrowing strategy, borrow and then pay back ahead of time—borrow again paying back early again—borrow more than before and again repay as early as possible but certainly on time. The strategy is to start with a relatively modest amount and build up a good borrowing and pay-back record, increasing the amount borrowed each time.

Two financial institutions that provide funds to businesses are banks and venture capital firms.

Banks

Much of your long-term and intermediate-term funding will come from banks. Bank loan officers will need to have much information about you and your firm before granting you a loan.

The loan officer will want you to prepare a detailed business plan, or projections which shows how the borrowed funds will be used, and a proposed repayment schedule. Your projections should indicate how the borrowed funds will benefit your business and increase profits.

The bank will check with other sources to determine your firm's ability to repay the loan. The loan officer will determine your character by asking people who know you such questions as:

☐ Are you managing your business effectively?

☐ Have you repaid your past debts?

☐ Are you basically an honest person?

☐ Do others trust you?

☐ Do you keep your promises to the best of your ability?

☐ What is the general outlook for your business?

The loan officer will also want to know your capacity to repay the loan. Although your management ability determines whether you are able to expand your business, the capital you have personally invested in the business will indicate your willingness to risk personal loss. The amount you have personally invested will indicate to others the extent to which you believe in the future success of your business. Additionally, the more successful you become, the more likely it is that banks will be willing to lend you money.

> Make a point of developing a long-term relationship with your banker. If he knows and trusts you, you will be more likely to receive a loan when you need it

Venture capital firms

In addition to banks, entrepreneurs may secure funds from a venture capital firm. A bank looks mainly at a company's ability to repay a loan, but a venture capital firm looks at the long-term future of the business. Venture capital firms become owners and buy stock in the company. Therefore, they are interested in the present and future products of a business and the size of present and potential markets.

Venture capital firms are chiefly interested in businesses having the future potential for achieving large profits. As a general rule, they look for three to six times their investment within six years. To obtain funds from a venture capital firm, you must start by submitting a well organised and well documented business plan.

The plan represents you and your company. It should contain your past accomplishments and show how your company has developed. Although the business plan contains the history of your company, it should also contain your future plans.

Analysing a business plan

Venture capitalists analyse very carefully the contents of business plans in order to identify the best possible investment opportunities. For every 100 proposals submitted by entrepreneurs for possible funding, only eight or ten proposals may be given careful consideration, and only one or two may be approved. Most business plans are prepared too quickly, with essential information omitted.

☐ Venture capitalists prefer to invest in businesses in specific growth industries because it will be easier for them to sell their financial interests in your firm at a profit. Make sure your proposal is considered by those interested in investing in your type of industry.

☐ If investors are interested in your industry, they will probably study your proposal. Your proposal should fully explain your company's position in the industry, your competition and your plans for increasing your share of the market.

☐ The proposal should arouse the interest of investors. Among the financial terms of the sale in your proposal, include the following items: (a) amount of debt or equity in your firm being sold; (b) allowance for partial purchases; (c) the types of ownership rights (common stock, preferred stock, straight debt, etc.); and (d) the total valuation of your firm after financing is secured.

☐ Potential investors will want to know the quality of the management staff, especially your qualifications as owner. Your board of directors, present investors and professionals associated with your firm should also be identified.

☐ Investors should get much information about the financial aspects of your firm by reading the balance sheet and profit-and-loss statement; make sure this information is accurate.

☐ Because your proposal is one of many received by venture capital firms, you must highlight the attractive features of your proposal.

Investors are looking for the best possible deal and you should be aware of the total value of what you are giving up in return for funds. Investors will demand as much as you can give in terms of: (a) interest on the invested funds; (b) a more favourable position than current stockholders if the firm is liquidated; and (c) large capital gains if the firm is profitable.

You should evaluate potential investors as carefully as they investigate you. Your ability to raise funds is an important factor in determining the type of business you enter, and its potential size. Your negotiating skills with the investors will determine your success in securing funds at a reasonable cost.

Contents of the business plan

The contents of the business plan should be well organised and well documented. Include information you believe a venture capital firm would need to make judgements concerning the investment possibilities of your firm. The business plan should include the following information:

☐ *General overview* (one-page summary). List your project idea, key goals and objectives, and financial requirements. Identify key financial facts from the previous year's operation, such as annual sales, net profit, number of employees, share of market and geographical location.

☐ *Past history*. Prepare a description of the past developments of your business, including product development, financial sources and organisational changes.

☐ *Describe products*. Prepare a full description (including costs and selling prices) of your present products. Identify special features that make your products unique. Identify plans to improve current products and to develop new ones. Describe pricing policies for products, including prices to distributors and their prices to consumers. Indicate how your prices compare with those of your main competitors, and how your products differ from those of competiton.

☐ *Market information*. Prepare a description of your current and potential market segment, unique features of the market, listing of competitors, and strategies for increasing your share of the market. Identify marketing objectives and strategies, including market research data. Include a sales analysis (in quantitative terms of units and currency) of products sold during the past few years by geographical areas.

☐ *Customers*. Give annual sales figures, details of special sales agreements, and other helpful information. Include background information regarding key customers if your sales are dependent on relatively few customers.

☐ *Industry competition*. Describe the present status and future potential of the industry. Identify growth factors. Identify competition within the industry and list your primary competitors. Indicate areas where your firm has a competitive advantage and where other firms have a competitive advantage over you. Identify your share of the market and the plans for expansion. Describe the potential for new product development, and identify technological trends in the industry which may have positive or negative effects on your firm.

☐ *Fixed assets*. Describe the buildings, machinery, equipment and other fixed assets owned by your firm, including age and depreciation. Identify production capacity and potential to increase capacity. Outline costs and potential methods of financing future capital expenditure.

☐ *Personnel data.* Give general information by department regarding number of employees, percentage of labour in cost of goods sold, special skills and salaries, employee morale and union influence. Include brief assessments of key employees. Indicate the extent of management ability of key personnel. Include an organisational chart to relate key personnel to job areas. List employee fringe benefits, such as pensions, profit-sharing, bonuses, hospitalisation, medical and life insurance.

☐ *Research involvement.* Give the expenditures and results of research and development during the past five years, and your current and future plans. Identify employees involved in research.

☐ *Business strengths.* Identify special aspects of your business which would make it attractive to potential investors: for example, you may have a long-term commitment from a customer to purchase products from your company.

☐ *Business weaknesses.* Identify potential liabilities, pending legal problems, tax concerns and other potential problems which might affect business operations. Be honest about your weaknesses because the potential investors will probably find them out anyway. Whenever you name a weakness, say how you plan to eliminate it.

☐ *Financial areas.* The financial condition of your business will be reviewed closely by *all* potential investors. Be careful to give accurate information and data about the financial condition of your business. So that the information is thorough and unbiased, you might engage an outside accounting firm to do the financial analysis. Include audited financial statements and comparative profit-and-loss statements from previous years, and financial projections for the next five years. Include tables and charts of sales, labour costs and administrative costs to illustrate trends in your business. The normal business ratios should be included and favourable ratios should be highlighted.

☐ *Financial needs.* State the amount of money needed from the beginning to the end of the proposed project, how the money will be used and the structure of the financial arrangements. Justify the amount requested. Describe other financing if your request is part of a larger financial package. Funds to be used for construction or capital additions should be justified with detailed cost estimates. Estimate how the proposed financing will increase earning power. If additional financing is needed during the next five years, identify amount, timing and your proposed method of finance.

To summarise, potential investors want to know as much about your firm as possible. Take care to develop a business plan that is comprehensive, well developed, logically organised, and presented attractively.

Remember, out of every 100 proposals submitted to a venture capital firm, no more than eight or ten will be of interest to them. After a second review, only one or two proposals may be seriously considered. Whether or not your business plan is accepted by a venture capital firm, the plan will help to organise the direction of your business for the next few years. The plan will help you to formulate long-range goals and make projections regarding the future

PERCEIVING MARKET OPPORTUNITIES

13

Many businesses offer good products; but unless the entrepreneur takes advantage of market opportunities, few of these products will be sold. Factors related to perceiving new marketing opportunities include conducting market research, gathering data from various sources and selecting a business location

Entrepreneurs have a constant need for information and knowledge about their markets. The purpose of marketing is to satisfy the demand of customers, and it is through research that you will be better able to make marketing decisions. Market research can help you to:

☐ find profitable markets;

☐ select saleable products;

☐ determine changes in consumer behaviour;

☐ improve marketing techniques; and

☐ plan realistic objectives.

The purpose of market research is to gather information to use in making decisions. Many entrepreneurs make the mistake of basing decisions on their own feelings and opinions. To be valid, however, your decisions should be based on the best information available. Market research will help you to identify new markets to enter, and to find new customers in your existing markets. You should know the reasons for your current products' success or failure, and have ideas about new products which have future potential.

Market research is the systematic gathering, recording and analysing of information about matters relating to the marketing of goods and services. Conducting market research to find answers to the following questions will help you to be more successful:

☐ What are the present and potential needs of your customers?

- ☐ What additional markets might be explored?
- ☐ What are the special characteristics of your customers?
- ☐ What makes your product or service different from those of your competitors?
- ☐ How effective are your promotional activities?

Market research attempts to evaluate your markets in a scientific manner. It is also an art, because it involves the constantly changing attitudes of people. By collecting marketing data in an orderly, objective manner, you will be able to know more about your markets. No matter what the size of your business, there is a need to determine the attitudes, opinions and beliefs of your customers.

Large businesses may hire marketing specialists; but as the owner of a small business, you probably cannot afford to hire marketing specialists. However, you should know your customers and be able to learn about their changing likes, dislikes and buying habits.

You can learn a great deal about your customers just by observing them. How do they dress? What are their ages? What is their marital status? How many have children? These questions are obvious, and most owners can get a feel for their customers by observing them. Keep records for a week and keep track of what you're able to tell about your customers from simple outward clues.

Market research provides the timely information and data you need to:

- ☐ reduce business risks;
- ☐ identify problems and potential problems in your current markets;
- ☐ identify new market opportunities; and
- ☐ obtain basic information and facts about your markets to help you to make better decisions and set up plans of action.

> Many small businesses concentrate on improving their methods of production. However, conducting research to make improvements in marketing your products may bring even greater benefits

CONDUCTING MARKET RESEARCH

You are probably involved in market research as part of your daily routine management activities without being aware of it. For example, you may be checking returned merchandise to see if there is a particular problem. You may be asking old customers why they have stopped making purchases from your store. You may study advertisements of competitors to see how they try to sell their products.

Market research simply makes this process more orderly. It provides a framework that lets you judge objectively the meaning of the information you gather about your markets. The following steps illustrate the marketing research process:[1]

- [ ] define the problem;
- [ ] conduct preliminary investigations;
- [ ] plan the research;
- [ ] use your own resources;
- [ ] use outside resources;
- [ ] interpret the data;
- [ ] make a decision; and
- [ ] implement and evaluate your decision.

Define the problem

The general problem must be clearly identified before the specific marketing issues can be determined, the research questions formulated, and the general types of solutions determined. Before conducting the research, you have to know what questions to ask. After stating your basic problem, try to identify all possible factors (in measurable terms) which may have caused or affected the problem.

Conduct preliminary investigations

An initial investigation will help you further to define your problem. Tentative solutions may also be developed and tested. Further study may identify other potential solutions. At this point, determine whether further research is necessary, and whether the potential outcomes would be worth the additional time, cost and effort.

Plan the research

By the time you begin planning the research, you should have a good understanding of the problem and the available facts which affect it. The problem and related facts will help you to determine the techniques to gather the data and find a solution. Data-gathering techniques include survey questionnaires, specialised quantitative techniques and market measurements.

---

[1] Adapted with permission from United States Small Business Administration: *Learning about your market*, Small marketers aids, No. 167 (Washington, DC).

The various kinds of market research include statistical analysis, sales analysis, surveys, observational research and experimental research.

Use your own resources

Before considering a market research study, look at the information that is available to you. Customer files and records may be very helpful. Study sales records, complaints lists, receipts and other cumulative records. This information can help to identify where your customers live and work, their buying habits, what they buy, how they buy, when they buy and where they buy. Maintaining good contacts with your market will help you to determine your customers' changing wants and needs. All this information costs little or nothing and can be of great benefit to you.

Your employees will also probably have valuable information about customers' attitudes and opinions. See that employees keep a written record of customers' complaints, items requested by customers that are out of stock, and comments by customers about your services. Talking with employees about *their* day-to-day contacts with customers may give you a different perspective on your marketing procedures.

Use outside resources

Once you have obtained information from sources within your organisation, you may need to seek sources outside your business. There is a great deal of published material relating to market research, including articles, printed surveys, magazines, published reports and books, all of which are called "secondary" resources. Secondary resources are available from libraries, government agencies, educational institutions, and booksellers and publishers.

Information gathered from secondary resources should be helpful in organising formal market research projects. These projects may result in primary research, which may be as simple as giving all customers who come to your place of business a questionnaire, and later summarising the results. More sophisticated studies can be designed and conducted by market research organisations, but the cost will probably be high.

Interpret the data

Although gathering the data is part of your market research activity, the effective solution to a marketing problem is determined by interpretation of the data. It is important to know the meaning of the data, and how they can be used in making informed decisions.

Make a decision

Your decision is affected by the interpretation of the data, but it is up to you to take into account all intangible factors and your personal opinions about the research study. If your feelings match the interpretation of data, you will be more confident in your decision. If your opinions differ from the interpretation of data, further analysis is necessary.

Implement and evaluate your decision

The final step in conducting market research is to implement your decision and evaluate the results. Only in this way can you accurately determine the effects of your decision. As a result of evaluating the results of your decision, you may have to conduct further studies. Your evaluation data may be used as input in conducting other marketing studies. In conducting a market research study, you may want to ask yourself the following questions:

- ☐ What are my business objectives?
- ☐ How would I describe my customers?
- ☐ What are my customers' views of my business?
- ☐ How would I describe my competitors?
- ☐ What is my product strategy?
- ☐ What is my pricing strategy?
- ☐ What is my promotion strategy?
- ☐ How do I justify the location of my business in terms of its ability to serve my customers?

One important decision is in the selection of products or services to be sold. Many small businesses are started because a need exists that is not being satisfied.

> In looking at a potential business, conduct market research to select a product or service that is essential to customers, and where a real need exists or can be relatively easily developed

INTRODUCING NEW PRODUCTS

Evaluating the potential success of a new product is a difficult but necessary activity. The following questions will help you to identify market opportunities for a particular product:

- [ ] Is the product in a growth industry?
- [ ] Will the future demand for the product increase, remain stable or decrease?
- [ ] What is the nature of your competition?
- [ ] To what extent are you dependent on suppliers and related businesses?
- [ ] Do you have sufficient finances to meet the expenses of introducing the new product for at least the first year?
- [ ] What are the specific disadvantages of the new product?
- [ ] In what ways will the product be similar to and different from those of your competitors?
- [ ] How can you increase the market area of the product?
- [ ] To what extent will marketing contribute to the success of the product?

Essentially, the basic function of business is to satisfy human needs. It is through research and product development that these needs can be identified, and goods and services can be produced and sold by business for profits

---

CENSUS DATA

Most governments publish statistics relating to the economic aspects of its people. This source of information is not used effectively by most entrepreneurs. Many of the statistics available are not directly related to your understanding of new market opportunities; however, these data will make you better informed.

Information about markets is essential to operating a small business and meeting competition from larger businesses. The census provides statistical input for solving problems which will help you to make decisions to increase the effectiveness of your marketing activities.

Census statistics are comprehensive and detailed; and you must interpret them. Stating your need for information in the form of questions concerning potential customers is a good way to organise your thinking. A sample question might be: "What geographical areas contain the best opportunities for new customers?" In working out an answer to this question, information extracted directly from the census tables can be immediately useful, such as population count, income, family size and occupation. These details are recorded for specific areas in a country.

Sales territories may be determined by the census data. Once sales territories are established, the census data can facilitate setting equitable sales quotas. A study of detailed census reports of employment levels, income and population density for each area of the territory of each member of the sales staff can indicate the potential sales.

Some products are included in the census. For example, the housing census may have statistics on home appliances, such as washing machines and refrigerators.

If there are no census figures for your type of product, you will have to use related data. Heavy concentrations of a certain product are also good prospects for a similar type of product, and you might make valid inferences about your market potential.

When introducing new products, you can use census data in two ways. First, new products may be suggested because the statistics reflect the *living patterns* of consumers. Second, the statistics may be used in connection with market testing. The census supplies demographic characteristics, such as age, sex, race and marital status, which can be helpful in selecting test market cities.

The experience of a small meat-packing plant provides an example of the use of census data in new product development. Its owner learned that the statistics for his sales area showed an impressive number of home freezers. In these he saw a new market—cuts of meat sold in bulk lots for storage in home freezers.[1]

Most countries have census data which may be useful in finding new marketing opportunities. Contact government agencies for information

---

Using the census data

Census data can help you to answer the following questions about your marketing procedures:

☐ What are the business and economic conditions in a particular geographical area?

☐ What cities are most appropriate for conducting marketing surveys?

☐ What are the key market areas for specific products?

☐ What are the incomes, buying habits and product preferences of people in a particular location?

---

[1] Adapted with permission from United States Small Business Administration: *Using census data in small plant marketing*, Management aids, No. 187 (Washington, DC).

- [ ] What factors will determine your marketing area?
- [ ] Where is the best place to locate your business?
- [ ] What are the specific characteristics of your potential customers?
- [ ] What is the employment status and occupation of people in a specific area?
- [ ] What are the income characteristics and spending habits of these people?

The census data may include detailed information about marketing in the retail, wholesale and service areas. This information includes sales, employment and payroll. The real value of this data is the manner in which it is evaluated and applied to your specific needs.

BUSINESS LOCATION

Location is important for some businesses, such as a clothing store or grocery store; but it is not as important for an antique store or motor car repair shop. Because it is difficult to relocate a business, be very careful in making this decision. Basic questions regarding location include:

- [ ] What part of the country?
- [ ] What city?
- [ ] What section of the city?
- [ ] What specific location in that section of the city?

The relative importance of location factors differs according to the nature of your business. In general, your location will be determined by:

- [ ] nearness to markets;
- [ ] relationship to customers;
- [ ] availability of qualified staff; and
- [ ] availability of raw materials.

The wider your market area, the less important your business location becomes. If your market area is small, your choice of business location will be more important. However, as a general principle, your business should be situated so that you have convenient access to your customers and your customers have convenient access to your business.

You should consult the following before making a decision about the location of your business:

- [ ] *Bankers.* They usually have a good understanding of the business conditions and the background of most business locations within a community.
- [ ] *The local chamber of commerce.* This could be of assistance in

Figure 19. Costs Analysis Form

Cost consideration	Location 1	Location 2	Location 3	Location 4
Purchase costs Land Building				
Operating costs Labour Power and heat Insurance Other				
Taxes Property tax Income tax Payroll tax Local tax				
Transportation From suppliers To customers				
Other _____ _____				
Other _____ _____				

recommending desirable locations, depending on your particular type of business.

☐ *Wholesalers, manufacturers and suppliers.* These have considerable knowledge about locations within a given market area.

☐ *Trade associations.* They have information about the economic conditions and markets within a specific area.

☐ *Government agencies.* Those which promote business development will be able to provide additional assistance.

☐ *Other sources.* These include industrial development areas, power companies, railway companies, real estate agencies, employment service offices and local businessmen.

In making a final decision, you may want to compare various sites. The major cost items for owning and operating a particular site might serve as a basis for comparisons. The Costs Analysis Form in figure 19 will enable you to summarise the information you need to make an informed decision. The completed form, with city and regional maps, and statistics concerning population and income, should help you to make the right one.

> To increase the chances of success, considerable thought should be given to the problem of selecting the right location of your business. A good location may allow a marginal business to survive, whereas a bad location may result in failure for even the best planned business

MARKETING THE PRODUCT OR SERVICE

14

No matter how good you are in all aspects of operating the business, you can't be successful unless you can sell your products. Business success is determined by customer demand

CUSTOMERS

Your business exists to satisfy your customers; your product or service must satisfy the needs of customers better than those of your competitors.

You must first identify your customers' needs, and then develop your product or service to meet those specific needs. Because of their size, it is not possible for most small businesses to spend large amounts of money to develop markets for their products.

Some entrepreneurs have started their businesses with products or services which they have developed or in which they have a deep personal interest. They may assume, incorrectly, that customers will want their products or services. This is the wrong approach for an entrepreneur to take because *creating a demand* will involve a great deal of time, energy and money.[1] If your business enters an existing market, most of your time, energy and money will be spent in finding new markets or persuading customers to change their buying habits and make purchases from your company rather than from your competitors.

Your product or service must provide customers with a better way of doing something. Because of the size of your business, you cannot sell to everyone. You must identify and focus on a specific part or segment of the

---

[1] See ILO: *Creating a market* (Geneva, 7th impr., 1980).

total market. A specific market segment (customers) can be classified by income, geographical area, sex, age, fashion or interest.

Because your business is totally dependent upon customers, you must do everything possible to react to customer wants and needs. The following trends will help you to identify changes in customer behaviour:

☐ Customer sales are an important indicator of success. Compare this month's sales with those for the same month last year. Watch for decreasing sales for the last two- or three-month period. It may indicate the beginning of a negative trend.

☐ Check for a decrease in credit purchases by regular customers, or a decrease in the number of new customers. Take action and talk to employees and customers to find out their attitudes towards your products or services.

☐ Increasing sales contacts with customers may have no effect on sales. Your sales staff should determine what is wrong.

☐ Purchase returns by customers may increase. Make inquiries of customers and employees to find out why this is happening.

Be aware of these indicators of customer attitudes to your products and services. Be quick to take action to reverse a negative situation, or a trend which involves decreasing sales.

Most small businesses cannot afford the research and development needed to put a new product on the market. Because marketing costs are usually high, you must determine whether you have the necessary resources to be involved in both new product development and the marketing of the new product. Most small businesses have limited finances and they cannot do both. Therefore, your expenditures for new product development and the marketing of new products should be minimised in most instances. Focus your efforts on established customer demands which are not being satisfied in the market.

A strength of small businesses is their adaptability to new market situations. Being flexible in your marketing efforts will help you to react to the changing demands of customers. Be selective in determining specific markets. Develop good relationships with your customers, and know the reasons why they give you their business.

> Introducing new products or services is beyond the capacity of most small businesses. However, small businesses can be competitive with innovations in production or distribution

PRICING

Pricing must be worked out to cover costs and provide a margin for profit. However, other considerations must also be taken into account; for instance, pricing your goods and services can be a real problem in cases where you have little competition or are selling a unique product or service. The price may have little or no relationship to your costs of production, and customer demand will help to determine your prices.

In most cases, your competition limits your ability to set prices. Price is a major factor when your products and services are similar to those of your competitors. Try to base your prices on some special feature or characteristic of your own product.

Price is not the only factor in determining sales. Providing various services to your customers—such as personal attention, free delivery and credit—and having a wide variety of merchandise may give you an advantage over your competitors.

Make sure that all departments of your business and all staff members are customer-oriented. Try to evaluate your customer relations periodically to determine specific ways to improve those which will result in increased sales.

Believe in the motto: "The customer is always right." Try to understand your customers and be interested in them. Customers buy where they feel welcome and receive good service

---

ATTRACTING NEW CUSTOMERS

For many small businesses, large expenditure on advertising may not be needed because most sales result from personal contacts within their community. Recommendations by satisfied customers are important to small businesses. Ask satisfied customers to recommend your business to other persons, or to give you the names of other people who could use your product or service.

Your business should have a trademark (or logo) which identifies your company and appears on all company signs, business cards and invoices, on company motor cars, vans and trucks, and on all business correspondence.

Employees can also help in locating new customers. They should understand that their jobs are dependent on the success of the business, and increasing customer sales will make their positions in the business more secure.

Entrepreneurs will make valuable contact with new customers through involvement in community activities. People appreciate any work you do on behalf of the community and may show their appreciation by becoming customers.

Media advertising to reach potential customers is usually expensive and not worth the cost. Advertising on the radio or in newspapers should be done on a small scale. The results of the advertisements, in terms of increased sales, should determine whether the advertising was worth the cost. Handbills are a means of giving a specific message to a special group of people. Sending printed advertisements by direct mail is another effective means of contacting specific potential customers. All printed materials which advertise your product or service should be attractively prepared: they represent you *and* your business.

> Don't wait for customers to come to you; go out and find them

PROMOTING YOUR BUSINESS[1]

You are the key person in any promotion effort and have the main responsibility for developing positive relationships between your business and the public. The reputation of a small business is usually directly related to the personality and actions of its owner—the entrepreneur.

You must identify specific customer groups, and inform them of your products and services through special promotions. When customers have confidence in you and your business, they will turn to you more and more to meet their specific needs.

Sales promotions are the *special efforts* you make to increase sales. A sales promotion may involve a special introductory offer, reduced prices, a demonstration, special displays, free samples or special advertising.

To promote your business properly, you must understand the market you are trying to reach. Know the characteristics of your customers, such as occupation, income, age category and special interests. Know who your customers are, where they come from, when they buy, what they buy and why they buy from you. Know the size of your current share of the total market. Make your sales promotions different from those of your competitors. Pay attention to effective promotions by competitors, and by businesses in other fields which are especially effective. Base your promotions on the real needs of your customers.

---

[1] See also Owen Dibbs and Patricia Pereira: *Promoting sales: A systematic approach to benefit selling* (Geneva, ILO, 1976).

Figure 20. Sales Promotion Chart

Type of promotion	Promotion costs	Dates of promotion	Sales during promotion	Sales of previous year
1.				
2.				
3.				

After defining your market, you need to determine the type of sales promotion you want to develop. When deciding what factors to promote, keep in mind the customers' basic reasons for buying. People buy because: (a) they want status (latest clothing fashions or furniture); (b) they have a basic need (food, shelter); (c) they have a desire for non-basic needs or luxuries (television set, cosmetics); or (d) they want to use products for business use (typewriter, van, desk).

The type and extent of your sales promotion will be determined by your responses to the following questions:

☐ What are your marketing policies?
☐ Where are your potential markets?
☐ Who are your sales target groups?
☐ What advertising media should be used?
☐ Is there sufficient money to conduct a successful sales promotion?
☐ When should the sales promotion be initiated?
☐ How can the outcomes of your sales promotion be evaluated?
☐ How are your special promotions different from your routine advertisements?
☐ How are your employees involved in the sales promotions?
☐ Does your sales promotion "sell" your business as well as a specific product or service?
☐ How can you measure the effectiveness of your promotion?

Certain factors about your business should be considered when you are deciding how much sales promotion is needed. For example, the longer you have been in business and the more successful you are, the less likely it is that you will need special sales promotions. New businesses, or businesses that have changed locations, need sales promotions to make potential customers aware of their existence. The type of your sales promotions will also be determined by your products (the more specialised the product, the more important are sales promotions) and your location (the more your business is removed from customers, the more you need to promote).

Results from your current sales promotion activity should be compared with the results of previous promotions. The chart in figure 20 may be helpful in determining the effectiveness of your sales promotions.

By monitoring your sales before, during and after a sales promotion, you will be able to measure its success. Comparing these sales figures with the previous year's figures will give you additional information.

> As a small business grows, it must expand its markets. Special sales promotions can provide the exposure that your product or service needs to increase sales in new markets

ADVERTISING

Advertising attracts customers and helps to get them to purchase your product or service. However, the quality of your product and service will determine whether or not they become regular customers.

Most of your sales are to regular customers; and the purpose of advertising is not only to attract new customers but to keep old customers as well. Advertising is a way to remind old customers and potential customers of your products and services.

Printed advertisements

Because many advertisements are in printed form, it is important to know the characteristics of this type of advertisement:

☐ It should be unique and distinctive.

☐ It should be simple and easy to understand.

☐ It should normally contain factual information which highlights one major point.

☐ It should project a very positive image of your company.

Most small businesses do not use advertising agencies to prepare their advertisements, but depend on their own personnel to develop ideas and prepare the "copy". Remember: keep your advertisement simple and to the point.

Many people read their newspapers for information concerning special sales; local newspapers, therefore, constitute a good advertising medium for small businesses.

The newspaper or radio station you propose to use for advertising may be able to help you to prepare a good advertisement. Advertisements in *official* telephone directories may be inexpensive but productive.

Evaluating your advertising

Advertising is very costly and must be used selectively by small businesses to achieve the best results. An evaluation of the effectiveness of an advertisement can be determined through research. To maximise your advertising at minimum cost, select a specific target group and use a specific advertising medium. How much a business spends on advertising is not as important as how the money is spent. A successful advertisement should result in increased income from sales which exceeds the costs of advertising. In addition to promoting a specific product or service, advertisements help to create the image of your firm.

Advertising assistance

Many entrepreneurs do not advertise because they do not have the time or skill to conduct a successful advertising campaign. Because you may be better at production than marketing, you may need outside assistance to develop your advertising programme. An advertising campaign has various integrated parts which must be co-ordinated and be given direction, and advertising specialists can be engaged to provide such assistance.

Commercial artists, copywriters, designers and advertising specialists offer their services on a fee basis. Often, their work is done on a part-time basis. Their services may be inexpensive because the work is done during their free time and they want to develop their own skills. They may be willing to work for you to have an opportunity to demonstrate their creative ability to develop innovative advertising ideas.

An outside advertising agency may assume complete responsibility for all your firm's advertising. The agency should be able to conceptualise, plan, organise, develop, conduct and evaluate an entire advertising campaign. Hire an agency that works in your specific marketing area, whether it be consumer, wholesale or industrial. Ask for references from former customers of the agency. Review samples of its work for other businesses and ask specifically about the benefits achieved (in terms of increased sales). Get the agency to prepare an outline of its projected advertising plan and give a detailed estimate of the costs.

Question any costs that you believe are too high and ensure that the agency justifies all costs.

Many advertising agencies have special agreements with newspapers or radio stations, receiving discounts when they place your advertisements. As your advertising programme increases, you may want to consider having an advertising specialist on your staff. This would allow you more direct control over the advertising programme. Advertising should be a continuous part of your business, and every phase of advertising should be related to the over-all direction of the total programmes.

In certain kinds of businesses, advertising assistance can be obtained from your suppliers. They may provide advertisements and promotional materials, especially for consumer-related products. Trade publications occasionally print articles and suggestions for advertising in a particular industry. Some trade associations have materials available for their members to help in the planning of advertising programmes.

> Advertising can attract potential customers to your business. However, it is up to you and your staff to make the sales and make them regular customers

FRANCHISING

Franchising is a system of distributing products or services through outlets owned by a franchisee, and it is one of the most rapidly growing areas of business activity. The franchise allows the franchisee to market particular products or services under a brand name according to specific terms and conditions.

One way for your business to grow is by selling franchises. In considering this distribution method, you may need to offer the following services to people buying your franchises:

- [ ] selection and purchase of location;
- [ ] construction of building;
- [ ] access to finances; and
- [ ] standardised procedures for all aspects of operating the business, such as accounting, management, advertising and production.

People interested in buying a franchise from you will want to know why your franchise is a better way to own a business than starting a business on their own. You should be able to answer satisfactorily the following types of questions:

Product considerations

- ☐ What are the current and the projected markets for your product?
- ☐ Who are your competitors; how does your product compare with other similar products?
- ☐ Is the product a fad or will demand for it be continuous?

Franchise contract

- ☐ Is the contract fair to both parties?
- ☐ Is the contract comprehensive; does it cover all aspects of the business?
- ☐ Are the purchase conditions for the franchise reasonable?
- ☐ Are the specific conditions in the contract reasonable, especially concerning: (*a*) fixed payments; (*b*) purchase of merchandise agreements; (*c*) sales quotas; (*d*) exclusive territory rights; (*e*) buy-back provisions; (*f*) termination of franchise agreement; and (*g*) total cost of franchise?

Franchisee assistance

- ☐ What types of training are provided to management and employees?
- ☐ What specific procedures are there for inventory control?
- ☐ What market surveys have been conducted?
- ☐ What are the provisions for advertising and special sales promotions?
- ☐ What financial assistance is available?

Market area

- ☐ How large is the franchise market area?
- ☐ Is the market territory large enough to support the franchise?
- ☐ What is the profit experience of the franchises in other territories?
- ☐ Do the financial statements indicate that the franchise is successful?
- ☐ Are statements of projected sales, operating expenses and net income available?

Franchising is a technique to use if you have developed a product or service but do not have the funds to market it successfully. Franchising your business allows your company to expand rapidly because most of the expansion costs are assumed by the franchisees. The franchise agreement should cover a specific time period. If the franchisee is not successful, you should have the option to terminate the agreement.

> Be careful to sell your franchises to well qualified persons because *your* success is dependent on *their* success

EXPORTING AND IMPORTING

The majority of export firms are small and this type of activity may create new markets for your firm. Exporting is difficult because you must become familiar with the laws, regulations, markets and business practices of another country.

Governments in all countries support exporting activities because it helps their balance of payments. There are government agencies in your country to help you to find markets and sales agents in other countries. If, on the other hand, you are establishing an *import* business, you can seek help from government agencies and exporting businesses in other countries. In some circumstances such help could include financial assistance.

If you plan to expand your business into exporting, you should first determine your potential production capacity. The difference between current production and plant capacity is the potential production available for export. Many of the business procedures are similar for domestic and foreign markets. Your biggest problems will probably arise through government regulations, language and the physical distance between you and your new customers. It may also be necessary to adapt your product or service and its means of promotion to suit new market conditions.

> Exporting may provide new markets for your product or service. Seek advice from government agencies about the opportunities

COMPETITION

Competition includes those businesses that sell similar products and services as well as other businesses that compete for the same customers. A restaurant owner competes not only with other restaurants but also with fast-food stands, grocery stores and open markets for the money customers have available to spend on food.

Your customers and potential customers have a choice; and you need to make sure that there are good reasons for them to buy from you.

Combining your own good ideas with the best ideas used by your competitors could give you an advantage. You can learn from your competitors' successes and avoid their mistakes. You must be prepared for constant change.

A single mistake can be disastrous to your business. You must be aware of what your competitors are doing. Knowing your competition helps you to understand the total business environment in which you operate. If you don't know how your competition will react to your plans for change, you are probably operating your business ineffectively.

There are various ways in which to obtain information about your competitors. Suppliers have information about the purchase of raw materials, or semi-manufactured parts or other materials, used by your competitors. Acting as a potential customer will allow you to discuss your competitors with suppliers. Suppliers will usually highlight the benefits of their products and explain how other businesses in the industry use them.

Some financial details about businesses are a matter of public information. These include special loans by government to small businesses, property taxes, or public corporations that must file certain forms giving financial data. Employees of your competitors may provide some information about their operations and activities which could be useful to you. Such opportunities to learn may arise during trade association or chamber of commerce meetings, when interviewing prospective candidates for positions, on social occasions, and the like. They may also turn out to be constructive critics by providing their ideas about how they feel you carry on your business.

But competitors are also trying to gain information about *your* business. Knowing what information might be valuable to a competitor, and developing procedures to keep this information confidential, should be standard practice in your company.

Attend professional meetings at which other entrepreneurs might explain some innovation or new management technique . Pay particular attention to successful owners. They are the people most likely to give such information and advice.

Taking business away from your competitors is one way to achieve growth. However, this situation may create problems for the entire industry. Your competitors will usually react quickly if they lose business to your company, and this creates an unstable situation in which problems are likely to occur. A better way to achieve growth is to expand your market. Rather than fighting competitors for the same pool of customers, concentrate on finding new customers. If you are competing in a market of many small businesses, such as restaurants or petrol stations, you can grow by introducing something new which makes your business different from the rest.

Another type of competition exists when a large firm dominates the market. In such cases you should avoid direct competition. Develop a product or service which complements those of your large competitor. It may be that you are able to compete with a large firm by offering your customers personal services and attention. Remember to concentrate on those aspects of business which your large competitor is not able to do as well as you. Many entrepreneurs do not speak to their competitors and may dislike them. This is a negative situation which you should avoid. Improving your own business should be your main goal.

In order to expand your business to serve a wider market, you may have to adjust your product design or marketing strategy. You may want to develop related products or a variety of models within your product line. You also may want to upgrade the quality of your products. This might increase sales to existing customers as well as attract new customers. You might consider avoiding your competition by introducing a new product which is not a part of your product line, especially if you can use existing manufacturing methods, equipment and channels of finance and distribution.

> As a general principle, it is more productive to concentrate on expanding your markets rather than competing with other firms for the same amount of business. Avoid conflicts with your competitors; they are not worth the trouble

OUTSIDE FACTORS

There are certain factors outside the firm that will affect the operations of your business. These factors may be outside your control but will influence your planning strategies. You should be able to forecast accurately the external factors set out in figure 21.

Laws have been introduced to protect consumers and to prevent unlawful practices within businesses. Be aware of these laws as well as new or proposed legislation which might affect the future operation of your business.

New technology can create problems if you have invested heavily in machinery and equipment which becomes out of date. Be ready to take advantage of new technology, as it becomes available, in order to become more competitive.

Up-to-date statistics and information about market trends can be obtained from government agencies. Trade associations and trade

Figure 21. External factors

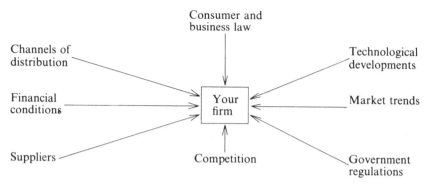

journals may be helpful. You must understand how new government regulations will affect your business.

Your competition changes as firms go out of business and new firms try to attract your customers. Competition exists for the materials you buy for making your products as well as competition for the products you sell. Trying to get the right quantity of materials at the right prices is a constant worry for most businesses.

Changing economic conditions will affect your firm. The financial aspects of your firm will be affected by the general state of the economy, the availability of money and the current bank interest rates.

You may use more than one marketing channel to sell your products. These channels are constantly expanding or contracting, depending on a variety of external factors.

The success of a small business can be greatly affected by factors outside the owner's control—factors to which you, as entrepreneur, must respond. You may not be able to avoid their influence. But you can lessen their impact if you act quickly and effectively

USING OUTSIDE RESOURCES

15

> Be with it! You never know when information you hear or read will help your business. Most information is free, but you must be smart enough to know where to look for it. In some cases you may have to pay professionals to provide help. Make sure that such help is worth the cost!

The failure rate for small businesses is extremely high, with most failing in the first few years. As an entrepreneur, you will face many problems which could be disastrous for your business. You will have to make many decisions on the basis of only limited information and understanding about specific problems. In many instances, information and assistance are available; but you may neither have time to learn about them nor be willing to take advantage of this help.

You cannot expect to have the best information and knowledge necessary for understanding and managing all aspects of your business. Large businesses usually have staff specialists to deal with such functional areas as marketing, finance, production and management.[1] However, as the owner of a small business, you must be knowledgeable in *all* aspects of your business. Because you may have few or no management support staff members within your firm, you should know about other sources of information and assistance. This chapter will help to identify potential sources of information and assistance, and give ideas about using them.

WHY LOOK FOR HELP?

Entrepreneurs value both their independence and their freedom to make decisions on their own. But, because decisions are best made after

---

[1] See Milan Kubr (ed.): *Management consulting: A guide to the profession*, op. cit.

considering all relevant information, there are times when outside resources should be used.

In practice, advice and suggestions from other people may be resented by some entrepreneurs. In your day-to-day business you probably receive advice from customers, employees, suppliers and competitors. You may think that there is no time to consult such people about your business problems. You may also believe that the effort needed to explain your situation to someone else is time which could be used to deal more effectively with day-to-day problems. However, you will collect a variety of ideas and opinions by discussing your problems with other people. Discussions with others are important for the following reasons:

☐ Information and ideas can come from many different sources. People view problems differently, depending on their positions, backgrounds and experiences. Discussing a problem with people having various viewpoints will give you new ideas for solving it.

☐ Contributions from a variety of sources should improve your decision-making ability. The more information you have, the better able you are to make an intelligent decision.

☐ Once you know how specific sources of information and assistance can help you, you are more likely to use these different resources in the future.

☐ When you demonstrate that you are interested in the ideas and suggestions of others, it is more likely that they will go out of their way to give you additional help and advice.

☐ When you realise that you do not have all the right answers, you will be more likely to listen to the ideas and opinions of others. Most entrepreneurs would increase their effectiveness if they improved their listening skills.

One of the entrepreneur's most important jobs is to *make decisions*. In smaller firms the entrepreneur usually makes all important decisions. Informed decisions are based on accurate information; and as their importance increases, the more likely it is that the information will not be available within the firm. Therefore, it is important for you to be aware of the many outside resources which can provide the essential information basic to decision-making

The less a decision has to do with the day-to-day operations of a business, the greater the need to seek the information from sources outside the firm

---

FREE ASSISTANCE OR FEE-FOR-SERVICE ASSISTANCE?

Some information and assistance will cost nothing; some you will have to pay for. Sources of free help include employees, customers, suppliers and other entrepreneurs. Help for which you pay a fee usually comes from lawyers, accountants, consultants and other "professionals".

Some sources of free assistance

Employees

Few entrepreneurs can do everything themselves. You must have qualified employees to relieve you of most day-to-day operational problems. This allows you time to work on long-term problems. The people who work for a business can provide answers to specific questions about it. For example, you might ask employees for their advice and assistance about items which are selling well, or stock displays, or customer attitudes. Your employees will give you valuable advice, provided that they know that their opinions and suggestions will be taken seriously.

Customers

Customers can supply very special information about the products and services they buy from you. You should ask customers for their opinions because they are an excellent source of information about the relative strengths and weaknesses of your business operations.

Suppliers

Because the success of most suppliers depends on the businesses they service, it stands to reason that they should be vitally interested in your success. Many suppliers are able to give you sound management advice because they can explain how other successful businesses operate. They can suggest ways for improving your business.

Other entrepreneurs

Some problems are common to most businesses, and entrepreneurs are generally willing to discuss their problems with one another. Occasionally, the competitive nature of business may discourage this frank exchange. If the businesses are unrelated, and do not compete for the same customers, the owners may be willing to share ideas to find

177

solutions to common problems. In this way, all entrepreneurs can benefit and improve their business operations.

Professionals

Formal consultations with "professionals"—bankers, management consultants, insurance agents, accountants, lawyers—involving the payment of fees for their services are dealt with later; but it is worth mentioning here that in informal discussion with them you can obtain much valuable information free of charge by asking the right questions.

Other sources

Besides people who can help you directly, there are many other information sources available to help to improve your business. Success or failure in using these outside sources depends on your ability to apply such advice and information in making effective decisions. Knowledge, ideas and information are valuable assets *only* if you can determine relationships between the knowledge and the needs of your business.

Keeping abreast of changes which will affect the growth of your business will not be easy; but the following are among the ways in which you can do so:

☐ *Industry data* will help you to compare your business with other similar businesses. The relevant information may be available from trade associations or government agencies and would include ratios such as stock turnover, cash discounts, percentage mark-up and average sales per month.

☐ *Membership of trade associations* will help you to contact other entrepreneurs throughout your country. Trade association services may include political lobbying, conducting research, organising education and training programmes, implementing new technology, responding to members' questions and concerns, and disseminating information through newsletters, magazines and special reports. Special groups such as employers' organisations can assist in counselling on industrial relations matters and in general public relations, whereas chambers of commerce and industry provide information and contacts for exports, arrange exhibitions, trade fairs and demonstrations and build up customer relations.

☐ *Subscribing to trade papers and magazines* is also desirable. You should set aside time to read items that are especially important in understanding new trends and developments relating to your business. You should maintain a file of pertinent articles for future reference.

☐ *Educational programmes* may help you to improve your management skills and ability. Training courses and adult education programmes have been designed by many institutions, agencies and associations for entrepreneurs. You should be aware of these personal development possibilities and take full advantage of them.

☐ *Consultants* can assist directly, in return for a fee, and indirectly, for no payment. Pay special attention to the approach and techniques used by a consultant to solve your business problems. When working on solutions to future problems, you may have to act as your own consultant and may want to use these same techniques.

☐ *The library* should be one of your primary sources of information. Government agencies have a variety of publications which may be helpful. Some colleges and universities maintain reference libraries which may be open to the public. Research institutes and some large corporations maintain libraries on specific topics. Trade associations and labour organisations may also have libraries containing material related to your specific needs. The library is a storehouse of information which may be useful to you in operating your small business. Books, periodicals, reports and newspapers may contain information which can help to solve some of the problems you meet in operating your business.

By talking to the librarian, you will know what free sources of information are available to you. If a library does not have a specific item, it may be able to get the material through what is known in some countries as the "inter-library loan" service. This service allows one library to borrow materials from another library. Obtaining statistical data, collecting facts and reading about business theory and practice can increase the probability that your business decisions will be based on fact rather than on opinion.

People who deal with your firm are your main sources of information. Pay attention to the opinions, suggestions and comments of your family, employees, customers and suppliers and other entrepreneurs. Printed information and data can be obtained from trade associations, government agencies, libraries, books, newspapers and magazines. Using these sources of information will increase your decision-making ability

---

Some sources of fee-for-service assistance

You can get fee-for-service professional help from people such as lawyers, accountants, insurance agents, bankers and business

179

consultants. The past performance of professionals with other entrepreneurs is a good indication of their future performance. Ask the advice of other entrepreneurs who have worked with consultants when looking for professional assistance. It may be that a professional you trust, such as a lawyer, can recommend a good accountant.

No matter what your needs, you should follow a standard procedure in selecting the best qualified professional. Once you have identified the best two or three qualified persons, you should arrange to meet them. Ask questions such as the following:

☐ How long have you been practising?

☐ What are your areas of specialisation?

☐ How have you helped entrepreneurs in a similar business with similar problems to mine?

☐ What are the names of some businesses you have assisted?

☐ How do you calculate your fees?

There is no way to be sure that you select the best professional to serve your needs. However, you should evaluate the work just as you do for your employees. Because these professionals are not a part of your regular staff, you should be able to terminate their employment if they do not meet your expectations. The more you know about your own business, the better you can judge the efforts of professionals. You must be willing to give them all the information they need to do their jobs effectively. The more complicated and specific your problem, the more you need assistance from a professional.

Lawyers

Because small businesses must comply with complex laws and regulations, you may need a lawyer to help with legal problems. Although laws and regulations are supposed to promote a smooth-running business system, they also, unfortunately, create many problems for most entrepreneurs.

You may not need a lawyer all the time, but you will probably require one at different times during the life of your business; and because you will have to develop a close working relationship with your lawyer, it is extremely important to choose the best possible lawyer to represent you. Interview several lawyers before choosing one. Ask for an estimate of fees for any activities planned to be carried out.

A lawyer's main job is to try to help you to avoid problems, but remember that they are usually conservative when giving advice. Their advice will usually concern those things *you should not do*. You should question their advice, and don't take their recommendations as sacrosanct. The lawyer should be able to give you various alternatives to a legal problem and be able to explain and justify the best alternative recommendation. Of all outside resources, your lawyer will probably be the person most negative toward your proposals and plans. In general, lawyers are very cautious people who are not risk-oriented. It is possible that you may want to give your lawyer stock or shares in your business rather than pay fees. This option will probably result in your lawyer taking a more personal interest in your business activities.

Most legal problems in a small business are routine and will not be very challenging to your lawyer. Nevertheless, it is up to you to make sure that you are represented properly. Most lawyers are paid on an hourly or daily basis, so it is important to make sure that you pay only for services provided.

Contact a lawyer when:

☐ signing a long-term contract;

☐ another lawyer representing another firm contacts you about a problem;

☐ planning to spend a large amount of money;

☐ you cannot reach a reasonable compromise about a business problem;

☐ making tax decisions;

☐ interpreting government regulations and laws;

☐ buying or selling stocks, bonds or other securities; and

☐ if someone claims you have acted in an improper, dishonest or illegal manner.

Most legal problems occur because of misunderstandings. If there is something you do not understand about your business dealings, it is best to contact the other party and discuss the misunderstanding before calling your lawyer. To avoid legal disputes, you should:

☐ deal mainly with people you know and trust;

☐ try to be fair and honest in all business activities; and

☐ put all important legal agreements in writing; oral agreements are difficult to enforce.

Your lawyer can provide a variety of services, including interpreting laws and contracts, to make sure that your business complies with the law. Since many major decisions have legal implications, you should talk things over with your lawyer before making such decisions.

Accountants

To make informed business decisions you must understand quantitative data. An accountant's job is to gather financial information about the past performance of a business, collate it, and assemble it in a form which can be easily interpreted. The past performance of your business is one of the best sources of information for making decisions about your company's future.

Depending on the needs of your business, it may be less expensive to hire an accountant on a part-time basis than to employ an accountant full time. When starting a business, an accountant will be most helpful in setting up an accounting system to meet the specific needs of the business.

You need to make a distinction between an accountant and a bookkeeper. The primary task of a bookkeeper is to record information and keep accurate records. A certified public accountant is a professional who has had years of training in interpreting financial data and has a certified licence to practise. As your business grows, your need for the help of a well qualified accountant increases. You will probably need a bookkeeper as well as an accountant.

Because most enterpreneurs are not aware of all the laws and procedures regarding taxes, a major task for an accountant is to make sure your business complies with the tax laws. Accountants should help you to interpret your financial statements and help you to *avoid* financial problems. Your accountant should not only provide information but also offer alternative strategies for improving financial planning.

A financial statement prepared by a qualified accountant is an opinion on the financial condition of a business. If you are expanding your business and need investors, you may want to have a well known, reputable accounting firm prepare an audited financial statement. People are more inclined to invest in a business if the audit has been carried out by a well known accounting firm.

Some large accounting firms have departments which specialise in providing management-type assistance to small businesses. The personnel of such a department would:

☐ advise and assist with the setting up of a small business, including its registration, forming a partnership or company, obtaining financial backing, and organising the financial framework of the business;

☐ design, initiate and maintain a complete set of financial records for the business—including routine and special financial reports;

☐ advise on finances in general and specific problems such as cash flow;

☐ develop and monitor credit systems;

☐ advise on cost control and pricing; and

☐ guide on tax matters.

Accounting consultants (financial advisers to entrepreneurs) should be able to provide advice and services relating to management, accounting and finance, as well as to make suggestions about business policies, procedures and operations.

Insurance agents

It is essential that your business has adequate insurance cover. Insurance helps to reduce extremely high risks, but you cannot insure against *all* risks (declining sales, for example).

Most businesses have some risks in common, including fire and theft. Other insurance cover is required by law, such as workmen's compensation insurance and motor vehicle liability insurance. The essential machines and equipment in your business should also have adequate insurance cover.

Insurance cover is necessary *only* for large potential losses. You must determine how large a loss you can afford without serious financial consequences. If your business is sufficiently strong, you may want only minimum cover against loss. Avoid spending money on insurance cover which offers no real benefits.

Try to think of new ways in which to reduce or avoid insurance costs. You may, for example, install an automatic sprinkler system or fire extinguishers, fire walls and doors, fire and burglar alarms and other safety devices to reduce risks as well as your insurance costs. Look for an insurance company which charges the lowest premiums but still provides you with the necessary coverage.

Be aware of your changing insurance needs by reviewing your policies at least once a year and making changes in coverage. Remember, as your business changes, so will your need for insurance.

Your insurance agent should make you aware of all possible areas of loss. However, the insurance company is the employer of the agent. It is up to you to make sure that the agent is interested in serving your needs rather than his own or the insurance company's needs. You need to find an insurance agent capable of providing the necessary services at minimum cost.

An insurance agent is, in effect, on the insurance company's sales staff. The more insurance you buy, the more money the agent will receive as commission. Buying too much insurance is just as bad as not having enough insurance. For example, insuring premises for $400,000 when their real value is $250,000 is wasteful, because if you make a claim the insurance company will pay only for actual loss (up to $250,000) and not up to the amount of your coverage ($400,000).

If you are the sole owner and manager of a business, your continued good health is of paramount importance. Your absence through illness (or death) would necessitate the appointment of a replacement. Money from insurance benefits could be used to hire someone with the requisite experience and skills to continue the business effectively.

Purchasing insurance is like purchasing all other items for your business. Obtaining bids for your insurance coverage from three or more insurance agents will help you to get a lower price. Your friendship with a particular agent should not affect your decisions. When updating your insurance each year, you may want to seek new bids from other agents.

Each agent should be allowed to determine your needs in detail. Because every agent will view your insurance needs differently, you will have a better understanding of the options available.

The nature of risks will vary according to your firm's location, facilities, products, services, customers and personnel. Some of the most common business risks include:

☐ Liability risks, such as: (a) a customer being injured on your property; (b) your delivery vehicle being involved in an accident; or (c) an employee being injured while working.

☐ Fire risks, which are determined by the cost of your buildings, type of equipment and volume of inventory. A fire may result in your business being closed for a period of time, which would mean a loss of business and a loss of customers. Fire prevention techniques to reduce your risk of fire would include the use of fire-resistant building materials, the installation of an automatic sprinkler system, and providing employees with information on how to prevent fires.

☐ Fraud and theft risks, which can be reduced by following good business practices. Hire employees that you can trust, and make sure your employees are aware of the various security practices needed to maintain control.

☐ Some risks which cannot be avoided, including storm damage and floods; and insurance may be the only way to deal effectively with these risks. Naturally, you should try to locate your business in an area with a low incidence of these types of natural disasters.

Because insurance can be highly complex and technical, you should deal only with a competent and professional agent. You need to discuss risks, cover, costs and other services which will provide you with the best possible business insurance programme. Choose an agent who understands the insurance needs of small businesses. Make sure you work with a full-time insurance agent. Don't deal with part-time insurance agents because you will probably receive only part-time assistance.

Bankers

A banker is a valuable source of assistance concerning financial affairs such as loans, lines of credit and operating ratios. Choose your banker carefully. In making your decision, have in mind a specific person working at the bank whom you trust and who has a great deal of banking experience. Discussing your financial affairs will be easier if you can provide your banker with a detailed business plan. Your business plan should be updated periodically and be discussed with your banker.

Your banker is an excellent source of information concerning the economic conditions and trends in your business area. Bankers can offer much information at little or no cost; thus, maintaining good relationships with your banker is essential. You may have borrowed money to start your business. As your business grows, so will your need for additional financial assistance. Bankers spend a great deal of time advising their customers on a variety of problems, most of which will relate to the effective use of money.

The assessment by a banker of your business strengths and weaknesses will help you to plan your future.

Business consultants

Because most small businesses do not have a large management staff, there are occasions when outside consultants are needed. These consultants should have a broad background in management, especially relating to small businesses. Although you can get guidance and assistance from consultants, it will be for you to make the final decisions concerning your business activities.

There are three broad types of business problems where using consultants is especially useful:

☐ a "one-time" problem, such as designing a new production system or conducting a market survey;

☐ a review of past business practices, such as a once-a-year review of the business; and

☐ a feasibility study, such as the location of a new store or a study of consumer acceptance of a new product.

Consultants may be useful for analysing and solving various management, operating and technical problems where you are not fully competent. The term "business consultant" should be used for people providing counselling services on a fee basis in such areas as accounting, advertising, data-processing, exporting, feasibility studies, financial control, industrial design, information systems, organisation, marketing, materials-handling, office systems, plant layout, production, public relations, staff motivation, training and recruitment, safety and finance.

Each of the above areas may require a different type of business consultant. However, not many entrepreneurs make use of business consultants. The reasons are many and include:

☐ a belief that consultant fees are too high;

☐ fear that consultants would give confidential information about their business to other people;

☐ the belief of owners that they are the only persons who can identify and solve their own problems; and

☐ a reluctance to gather the information needed for the consultant to do the job properly.

For these and other reasons, many entrepreneurs are not aware of the costs or benefits of business consultants. Business consultants should be viewed as another resource; and, as an entrepreneur, you should have experience of working with consultants before judging their value.

Before selecting a consultant, you should:

☐ know exactly what specific tasks you want the consultant to accomplish;

☐ gather information on the services offered and the general reputation of various consultants from your business acquaintances. Get each potential consultant to provide you with current references;

☐ know the specific areas of business in which each consultant is especially competent;

☐ make sure, when considering a large consulting firm, that you talk to the persons who will actually be assigned to work with you; and

☐ ask each consultant to prepare a written proposal that indicates the work tasks; how they will be accomplished; how long it will take to complete the job; an outline of the final written report; and an estimate of the total cost to complete the assignment.

You can pay consultants in various ways. You may hire consultants either on a fixed-fee basis or on a retainer basis. The retained consultant is available to your business at any time during the contract period, which may be for three months, six months, one year or longer. You or the consultant may want to base the fees on tangible results, such as higher sales, lower production costs, or a reduction in overhead costs.

Consultants provide special services to a business. Large firms hire consultants to solve technical problems or improve specific operations in such areas as finance, management, production or marketing. The need for consultants may be even greater for your small business, but your ability to pay for these services is less.

Because you are mainly concerned with day-to-day business affairs, you may be too close to your business to identify major problems—you may not be able to see the wood for the trees. Consultants can provide a broader perspective, give you new ideas, and use their past experience and knowledge to make suggestions which will improve your over-all business. Consultants can also help to implement recommendations which it may not be possible for the entrepreneur to accomplish alone.

The services of a management consultant should be regarded as an investment in the future. Making improvements in two or three areas of your business can result in significant future profits or savings. The services of consultants are essential to help entrepreneurs to solve problems and to prevent potential problems by identifying and eliminating their causes.

Owners of small businesses have limited staff, limited time and limited money. Yet the need for information and advice is continuous. Look for information and assistance from various resources outside your business: bankers, lawyers, accountants, insurance agents, consultants, suppliers and customers. Be a good listener and actively seek out the advice of these people. You do not necessarily have to follow their advice but you will gain a better understanding of your business situation. Outside assistance can help you to solve existing problems as well as to avoid potential problems

DEALING WITH GOVERNMENT AGENCIES

16

> Various government agencies regulate, monitor and provide assistance to small business. Knowing your legal rights and responsibilities will help you to maximise benefits from government agencies and minimise your obligations to them

GOVERNMENT AND SMALL BUSINESSES

National governments are becoming more interested in ways to assist their small business sectors. In the past, such assistance has been financial, technical and managerial.

Government, usually the largest single purchaser within a country, can ensure that certain purchasing orders are given to small businesses. Alternatively, a government might set aside a percentage of purchases to be awarded to small businesses for specific products and services.

Small businesses can sometimes pool their resources to bid for a government contract, because government agencies realise that it is important for small businesses to compete with large businesses. The small business sector must voice its concerns to government before government can be sympathetic to its needs. However, there is a reluctance on the part of owners of small businesses to organise and present their needs to government.

Within a government ministry, such as the ministry of commerce, an agency may be established to promote the interests of the small business sector. This agency may have the power to give financial assistance in the form of loans or guarantees for loans from other lending sources. These loans might be used to start a business or to expand a business. Loans may be given to special groups of people, or to help to remedy the effects of certain types of disasters beyond the control of entrepreneurs. In many rural areas government supports small businesses because they provide the bulk of employment opportunities outside farming.

LICENCES AND REPORTING

You will probably be required to obtain a government licence to operate your business. The government departments involved may be at the local, state, provincial or national level. Many entrepreneurs feel that the paperwork and licensing schemes seem designed to create unproductive work. However, licensing requirements help to prevent illegal practices by regulating the business system to operate effectively for the benefit of business as well as consumers.

While national development goals in most countries are expected to encourage the growth of small businesses, government regulations may actually serve as disincentives. Compliance with laws and regulations require businesses to file numerous statistical and other reports concerning their activities. The most important local and national government laws and requirements cover such matters as granting licences to operate businesses; zoning restrictions; building codes; taxes on property and income; sales taxes; corporation taxes; and contributions to health and unemployment schemes.

> To keep up to date on new or changed regulations, contact your local government agencies or seek assistance from your advisers

TAXATION

Prepare a worksheet to list your tax obligations. Because direct taxes must be paid at different times of the year, the worksheet can help you to identify potential cash-flow problems caused by tax payments. Figure 22 shows the headings that can be used in a worksheet for tax obligations.

The following suggestions should be helpful in managing your tax records:

☐ Keep written records of all financial transactions. These will help to determine your tax liabilities.

☐ Pay your taxes by cheque so that you will have proof of payment.

☐ Prepare a worksheet as shown in the example above.

☐ Pay your taxes when they are due, in order to avoid penalties or fines.

☐ Make sure the information in the tax reporting forms is accurate.

Figure 22. Tax Obligations Worksheet

Type of tax	Necessary forms	Due date	Amount due	Payable to	Cheque no.	Possible penalties for late payment

Treat tax obligations like any other business activity. The various government tax agencies should provide you with all the necessary information and forms. You may find it necessary to hire a special tax consultant to interpret the forms and provide advice about meeting your tax obligations and legally minimising your payments

BUSINESS LEGISLATION

Specific laws exist which affect business activity. The effects of these laws may differ from one country to another. In general, business regulation by government *increases* as the business sector expands.

Workmen's compensation is a form of insurance for your employees in the event of work-related accidents or illnesses, and its purpose is to protect and provide a sense of security for workers. Your premium for workmen's compensation may be based on your accident record, and premiums decrease if you have an effective safety programme which keeps work-related accidents to a minimum. It is therefore in your best interests to have a safety programme to protect the health and welfare of your employees. Safety legislation helps to ensure that the workplace is safe and not detrimental to the health of employees. As the employer, you are ultimately responsible for your employees' health and safety.

Legislation regarding wages and hours has been enacted in many countries. There may be a minimum wage for particular types of employment, and extra wages for overtime work. Employees may not be able to work beyond a certain number of hours per day or per week. These laws have been implemented to protect employees from exploitation.

Legislation allowing unions and collective bargaining will affect your business activities. Be sure to follow regulations regarding employees' rights to organise and belong to unions. Government agencies may help to settle disputes between labour and management.

As an employer, you may have the responsibility for collecting various taxes. Make sure you keep accurate records and follow appropriate procedures.

Some governments have enacted legislation covering the minimum age of employees, especially for certain occupations or industries which may be considered hazardous. Many governments have passed legislation to protect the environment from pollution. Your business may have to conform to regulations regarding air, water, noise and waste disposal.

Government agencies will be involved in regulating and monitoring your business activities in connection with safety regulations; food and drug laws; the formulation of partnership and corporation agreements; special licences; patents and copyrights; public sales of stock; franchise agreements; the resolution of labour disputes; and the sale or merger of a business.

> Although laws and regulations may appear to be government interference in business, they are imposed for the benefit and protection of both business and consumers

FORMS OF OWNERSHIP

Being and staying in business requires skill, strategy and planning. You also must understand the rules and regulations by which you do business. Before starting a business you must choose the legal structure that will best suit the needs of your particular business. Your planning must consider the various local, state, provincial and national laws that govern the operation of a business. To select the legal structure for your business, you should first know your alternatives.

There are three basic kinds of business organisations: the sole proprietorship, the partnership, and the company or corporation. Each has general advantages and disadvantages. The type of business organisation you choose will determine the special types of relationships you have with various government agencies.

Sole proprietorship

The sole proprietorship is the most widespread form of small business organisation in which the business is owned and operated by one person. To be a sole proprietor, you usually need only to obtain a licence or register a business name to begin operations.

Advantages of sole proprietorship

☐ The organisation may be informal, with few legal obligations. Little or no governmental approval is required, and it is usually less expensive to form a sole proprietorship than a partnership or corporation.

☐ The owner is not required to share profits with anyone.

☐ There are no co-owners or partners to consult (except possibly your spouse). Therefore, an owner will have complete control and decision-making power.

☐ The owner is able to respond quickly to business needs in the form of day-to-day management decisions.

☐ The sole proprietorship is relatively free from government control and special taxation.

Disadvantages of sole proprietorship

☐ The individual proprietor has unlimited liability and is responsible for *all* business debts. These may exceed the proprietor's total investment in the business. His liability extends to all his assets, including his house and other possessions.

☐ There will probably be less capital available than in other types of business organisations.

☐ The sole proprietor may have difficulty in obtaining long-term financing. To a great extent, the business is dependent on the skills of the owner. Consequently, the enterprise is unstable because illness or death of the owner will severely damage the normal operations of the business.

An entrepreneur might begin as sole proprietor and, if successful, develop the business into a partnership or corporation.

Partnership

A partnership may be defined as an association of two or more persons to act as co-owners of a business for profit. Articles of partnership are customarily drawn up to define the contributions by the partners to the business, and the role of each partner in the relationship. The following are typical articles to be found in a partnership agreement:

Name, purpose, location
Duration of agreement
Performance by partners
Nature of partners (general or limited, active or silent)

Contributions by partners (at inception, at later dates)
Business expenses (how handled)
Authority (individual partner authority in conduct of business)
Books, records, method of accounting
Division of profits and losses
Withdrawals of cash and/or salaries
Death of a partner (dissolution and winding up)
Management
Sale of partnership interests
Arbitration
Additions to or modifications of partnership agreement
Settlement of disputes

Some of the characteristics that distinguish a partnership from other forms of business organisation are the limited life of the partnership, unlimited liability of at least one partner, co-ownership of the assets, share in management, and share in partnership profits.

Advantages of the partnership

☐ Legal formalities and expenses are few compared with the requirements for the creation of a corporation.

☐ Partners are motivated to apply their best abilities because they directly share the profits.

☐ In a partnership it is often possible to obtain more capital and a better range of skills than in a sole proprietorship.

☐ A partnership may be relatively more flexible in the decision-making process than a corporation.

☐ The partnership is relatively free from government control and special taxes.

Disadvantages of the partnership

☐ There must be unlimited liability for at least one partner.

☐ The partnership ends when any partner dies or wants to dissolve the partnership. However, the business can continue to operate on the basis of right of survivorship and possible creation of a new partnership.

☐ It is relatively more difficult for a partnership to obtain large sums of capital, particularly for long-term financing, than for a company or corporation.

☐ The partners are agents of the business and their acts are binding on the other partners as well as on the business.

☐ There is difficulty in disposing of a partnership interest. The buying out of a partner may be difficult unless it is specifically arranged for in the written partnership agreement.

Company or corporation

This is by far the most complex of the three types of business organisations. It may be defined as "an artificial being, invisible, intangible, and existing only in contemplation of the law". In other words, it is a distinct legal entity and has a separate identity from the individuals who own it.

A company or corporation is usually formed by the authority of a government agency, and must comply with the laws regarding commerce, and with provincial and local laws which may vary considerably from one place to another. The procedure usually required to form a company or corporation is, first, that subscriptions to capital stock must be taken and a tentative organisation created; and second, that approval must be obtained from the government. This approval is in the form of a charter for the company or corporation, stating the power and limitations of the particular enterprise.

Advantages of the company or corporation

- ☐ The stockholder's liability is limited to a fixed amount, usually the amount of the stockholder's investment.
- ☐ Ownership is readily transferable from one person to another.
- ☐ The corporation has a separate legal existence.
- ☐ There is a certain amount of stability and relative permanence of existence. For example, if the chief executive dies, or simply disappears, the company or corporation can continue to exist and do business.
- ☐ It is relatively easy to secure capital in large amounts and from many investors. Capital may be acquired through the issue of various stocks and long-term bonds. It is relatively easy to secure long-term financing from lending institutions by using corporate assets as security.
- ☐ Owners delegate authority to professional managers who are specialists.
- ☐ The corporation can afford to employ specialists.

Disadvantages of the company or corporation

- ☐ Activities are limited by charter and by various laws.
- ☐ There are extensive government regulations to be observed, and burdensome local, state and national returns to be made.
- ☐ It costs more money to form a company or corporation than a partnership.

☐ There may be large taxes due to various government agencies.

Answer the following eight questions if you are forming a business organisation or are thinking of changing your current form of business ownership:

☐ To what extent are the investors liable for debts and taxes?

☐ What legal organisational form would ensure the greatest flexibility for management of the firm?

☐ To what extent would your country's laws and regulations affect the organisational form?

☐ What additional capital will be needed in the near future?

☐ What additional top management personnel will be needed?

☐ What are the costs and procedures to start the business or change its present form?

☐ What is the ultimate goal and purpose of the business?

☐ Which legal organisational form can best serve the purposes of the business?

> To some extent, government regulations and taxes influence the legal structure of your business. Review this legal structure each year; and make changes when the advantages of change are greater than the disadvantages